Passion for Justice

David Adam ◆ Joan Chittister
Thomas Cullinan ◆ Margaret Hebblethwaite
Mary John Mananzan ◆ Jon Sobrino

Passion for Justice

Reflections on the
Scripture Readings for Lent

The CAFOD/DLT Lent Book 1998

First published in 1997 by

CAFOD
Romero Close
Stockwell Road
London SW9 9TY

Darton, Longman and Todd Ltd
1 Spencer Court
140-142 Wandsworth High Street
London SW18 4JJ

Editors: Harriet Paterson, Eldred Willey

ISBN 0 232 52257 X

Cover: Painting of Christ in a church in Olinda, Brazil.
Photograph by Carlos Reyes-Manzo

Bible quotations are taken predominantly from the Jerusalem
Bible, published and copyright © 1967, 1968, and 1969 and the
New Jerusalem Bible, published and copyright © 1985 both by
Darton Longman and Todd Ltd and Doubleday and Co Inc.

Printed by Flexiprint Ltd
1 Aspen Court
Churchill Industrial Estate
Lancing, West Sussex BN15 8UN

Contents

About the authors

Jon Sobrino is one of Latin America's most eminent theologians. A Jesuit from Barcelona, in 1956 he moved to El Salvador and joined Archbishop Oscar Romero at the forefront of the struggle for justice. He is Director of the Archbishop Romero Pastoral Centre at the university in San Salvador, and is author of *Christology at the Crossroads*, one of the most significant works of liberation theology. Other books include *The True Church and the Poor* and *Jesus in Latin America*.

Margaret Hebblethwaite, assistant editor of *The Tablet*, is a journalist and author with an interest in Latin America, feminist theology and spirituality, and basic ecclesial communities. Her books include *Motherhood and God*, *Finding God in all Things* and *Basic is Beautiful*. She has been involved in a number of lay ministries and is currently Catechist at Exeter College, Oxford. Her late husband was the Catholic writer Peter Hebblethwaite, and they have three children.

Thomas Cullinan is a Benedictine monk of Ampleforth Abbey. He is part of a monastic presence near Liverpool, trying to respond to justice and planetary issues of our day. He has stood on Oxfam's Council and the Bishops' National Justice and Peace Commission. He is author of various articles and books including *If the Eye be Sound* and *The Passion of Political Love*.

Mary John Mananzan is a Benedictine Sister and is at present President of St. Scholastica's College in the Philippines. Director of the Philippine Institute of Women's Studies, she is currently Executive Secretary-Treasurer of the Ecumenical Association of Third World Theologians (EATWOT). She is the author of *The Language Game of Confessing One's Belief*, *The Woman Question in the Philippines* and numerous articles.

Joan Chittister OSB is a renowned international author and lecturer and founder/Executive Director of Benetvision: A Resource and Research Center for Contemporary Spirituality, based in Pennsylvania. Her bestselling books include *The Seasons of Life: A Time for Reflection*, *The Rule of Benedict* and *The Psalms, Meditations for Every Day of the Year*.

David Adam is the Vicar of Holy Island, where he meets thousands of pilgrims every year. He teaches and leads retreats both on the island and around Britain. A well-known author and expert on Celtic spirituality, his works include *The Edge of Glory, The Cry of the Deer, Tides and Seasons* and *Powerlines*.

Introduction

Lent is a season of renewal, a special time of conversion to the ways of God. We are tempted to think of it as a period of withdrawal, of seclusion, of escape. We sometimes think of conversion as a mysterious, essentially private activity, that cannot be engaged in by busy people all the year round, but which one tries to make space for at Lent: perhaps by "giving something up", by going to church more often, or by reading a book of reflections such as this one.

Lent *is* a special time of interior renewal, of rest and recreation for exhausted spirits. But it is more than this. As Joan Chittister writes, Lent is "that time when we ask ourselves what it is we are really doing with our lives".

The recurrent theme of the reflections in *Passion for Justice* is that Lent is a time, not purely of withdrawal and escape from the world, but of special alertness and readiness for involvement in God's creation. Lent is a time, not for our eyes to be turned away from the world, but for them to be focused on it with fresh awareness and understanding.

"Stay awake", the Gospel repeatedly warns us. Stay alert to the presence of God in all things. Lent is a special time for seeking out the things of God, and they are to be found not only within our hearts, but in every nook and cranny of our world. God's covenant is with the whole of creation. We do not need to retreat to a quiet space to find the stuff of conversion and renewal. God is present in our joy and despair, in our friendships and in our enmities, in our workplace, in our society, and in all the earth's structures and systems.

In conversion, we are searching for the wholeness that only God can give us. The Gospel shows us a God of love, of compassion, and of justice. In living out the Gospel we try to bring together contemplation with action, prayerfulness with the promotion of justice, conversion of heart with the transformation of creation.

We are growing closer to the dawn of the third millennium. Renewal and conversion are at the centre of the Church's preparations for this "great jubilee". We are living in a special time of re-commitment to the jubilee values of repentance and reconciliation. "In a world marked by conflicts and intolerable inequalities," Pope John Paul has written, "a commitment to justice and peace is a necessary condition for the celebration of the jubilee" (*Tertio Millennio Adveniente*).

What should we do with our lives? Where, amidst the babel of images and words of the modern world, do we find God? The Gospel finds the answer in poverty, in humiliation, in powerlessness. To love God, we are invited not only to serve the poor and the outcast, but to live beside the poor and the outcast.

Yet Lent is not a time for a busy, effortful lurch in a new direction. True conversion changes everything, inside and out. But it is not of our own making. Conversion is not a transformation we can control or shape. It comes only from letting go, from allowing control of our lives to pass from our own hands into the hands of God.

Conversion to the way of the Gospel is not easy or cheap, and often it is not gentle. Many of the reflections in this book look at renewal and conversion through the eyes of the poor and the marginalised. They come from the lived experience of poverty and oppression, where to speak words of truth and love risks persecution and even death, and they sing with a passion for justice.

Brendan Walsh

Jon Sobrino
Ash Wednesday to Saturday after Ash Wednesday

Ash Wednesday

How to become human

Jl 2:12-18; Ps 50:3-6, 12-14, 17; 2 Co 5:20-6:2; Mt 6:1-6, 16-18

"But now – declares Yahweh – come back to me with all your heart."

(Joel 2:12)

In today's world we celebrate many events: Independence Day, Mothers' Day and many other special occasions. However, has no-one ever thought of celebrating "Conversion Day"? These days we need to be converted, not only to be Christian, but simply to be human. Have not even the massacres in Rwanda, nor the poverty of three thousand million human beings, brought home the need for change in each and every one of us?

God thinks differently. He tells us: "Rend your hearts." Throughout the ages our Christian Churches have rarely welcomed the word of God. After all, it puts demands on them as well. At least the Churches have not dared to silence it, and every year, during Lent, they offer us time to think about conversion.

We have to be thankful for that, given that we live in a world of injustice and cruelty, where the seven richest men have enough wealth to wipe out poverty within a few years. A world where a footballer, a boxer or a singer earns more than entire towns and villages in Asia, Africa or Latin America and in which they are better known and more admired than the countless martyrs who have given their lives for love.

We live in a world where existence has been trivialised, where the tragedies of injustice are covered up. It is as if nothing serious ever happened in our lives; as if being human didn't have much to do with honesty, with seeing things as they are.

Joel, Jesus, and the martyred archbishop Oscar Romero are all right, despite the little attention paid them by Wall Street or the United Nations Security Council. We have to start by accepting that we have hearts of stone and ask for them to be made flesh.

Ignacio Ellacuria, the rector of the University of Central America in San Salvador who was murdered along with five other Jesuits, was right in his last speech he gave. In Barcelona in November 1989, a week before his death, he said: "We have to turn history around." In words that few would dare speak he said: "Today's civilisation of abundance must become a civilisation of poverty."

Thought for the day

In a world like ours, we truly have to "rend our hearts".

Prayer

O Lord, I acknowledge my guilt; create in me a new heart, and renew a steadfast spirit within me.

Amen.

Thursday after Ash Wednesday

Choose life

Dt 30:15-20; Ps 1; Lk 9:22-25

"Today I put before you life and good, death and evil."
(Deuteronomy 30:15)

With these words God reminds us of the seriousness of our lives and he orders us to choose between life and death – solemn words not often pronounced in a world which only seems to give us the choice between entertainment and making money.

The fact that good and evil exist, that we can give life or death to others – these alternatives are of interest to God, because he cares about us and wants us to have life.

But he doesn't deceive us, as advertising does, and so he reminds us that we have to choose. One might say that everyone wants life, not death. But it is not just a matter of wanting it, but of choosing the path that in reality leads to life or death.

St Ignatius of Loyola, as early as the sixteenth century, sensed the reality of "modern humanity". He said something which is not often heeded today and which carries little weight with that same modern individual.

He explains that there are two paths in life. One leads step by step to death. These steps are: first, riches; second, the honours bestowed by a sinful world; and third, arrogance.

The other path is that of good, the way of Jesus which leads to life. The first step is poverty; the second, rejection by the sinful world; and the third, humility, profound honesty and the freedom it brings with it.

St Ignatius insists on the good news that it is possible to live in this world as a human being and a believer. It is possible to live in truth in this world of lies, to live in justice in this world of oppression.

Nevertheless, Ignatius insists that we have to choose and that choice is "a duel", for one possibility fights against the other. We must be poor and struggle against wealth, be meek and struggle against the lure of power. We must be humble and struggle against arrogance. "Conversion" humanises us.

It is so important not to stray off the road that leads to life. Jesus spoke very simply about the true life: "Blessed are the poor, for theirs is the kingdom of God; but woe to you wealthy for you have already had your comfort."

Thought for the day

A Christian can bring cheer to the poor, but cannot congratulate a millionaire.

Prayer

Lord, in this world of selfishness, help us to live in solidarity.

Amen.

The origin of death

Is 58:1-9; Ps 51:3-6, 18-19; Mt 9:14-15

My offences truly I know them.

(Psalm 51:3)

Neither our lives nor our deaths are for ourselves alone. By our life others live and by our death others die. It used to be said that "mortal" sin brings death to the soul; but we have to add that such sin is "mortal" above all because it brings death to others.

This is clear in God's commandments. As we fulfil them, we receive life and give life to others; but when we break them, we bring death and we also die as humans.

So how does sin progress? In which order are the commandments violated? The origins of human sins are undoubtedly many. But in our present world the New Testament statement that "the love of money is the root of all evil" is illuminating. The process of sin begins with the violation of the seventh commandment, with stealing, depredation, plunder and injustice.

From there we go to the violation of the fifth commandment by murder, torture and massacre. For it may be necessary to murder in order to keep what was illegitimately stolen. And from there – to hide or even justify these violations – we break the eighth commandment, thou shalt not lie. When you deprive others of life, and the basic requirements for living, then you also lie to hide what you have done.

This happened, for example, when Europeans invaded other continents to enlarge their own empires. Then, in their version of events, the subjugated peoples were painted as villains and themselves as heroes.

In modern western cultures, even those with a religious basis, it becomes ever more difficult to keep to the first commandment: "You shall not worship false gods". As Jesus says, "No man can serve two masters, God and riches." With that we are back to the origin of sin: stealing.

When we accumulate riches, we are gradually or violently depriving other human beings, our brothers and sisters, of life. Expressed more strongly, we are bringing death.

Thought for the day

We shouldn't want to be better off, because effectively that means death to others. We should want to be worse off, so that everyone can live.

Prayer

Have mercy on me, Lord, in your kindness, in your compassion wash away my guilt.

Amen.

Saturday after Ash Wednesday

A shared table

Is 58:9-14; Ps 85:1-6; Lk 5:27-32

*At the table with them were a great number of
tax-collectors.*

(Luke 5:29)

The gospel tells of the conversion of Levi the tax-collector:
"Leaving everything, he got up and followed Jesus." But this
is followed by a banquet. In Lent we certainly must
remember the "conversion", but we should also highlight
the rejoicing that accompanied it.

Jesus gives dignity to the sinner, the one scorned by
religious people of the time. He says tenderly to the sinning
woman prostrate before him: "Your faith has saved you." He
does not take credit for himself but gives it to the sinner. The
gospel goes on to narrate the joy of Jesus at the banquet with
the tax-collectors.

The "shared table" was essential for Jesus and for the first
Christian communities. There is certainly an ethical
dimension here – sharing with others – and also a liturgical
one – celebrating the Lord's Supper. The question for the
Church has been with whom to share the table. Sometimes
it does it right, sometimes not. Let's look at two examples.

Eusebius of Caesarea, the chronicler of the early centuries of
the Church, describes the banquet which concluded the first
Council of Nicaea in AD325, when nothing less than the
divinity of Christ was proclaimed. "The Emperor invited
God's ministers to a banquet which was sumptuous beyond

all expectation. Detachments of soldiers stood guard at the entrance to the palace, sword in hand, and walking between them, the men of God proceeded fearless into the Imperial reception rooms; there some joined the Emperor at the table, while others reclined in armchairs on both sides . . ." This was not how Jesus shared his table!

Rutilio Grande was a Salvadorean Jesuit who was murdered in March 1977. He was shot as he drove from the village of El Paisnal to Aguilares. His death was a turning point in El Salvador, the catalyst which converted Archbishop Oscar Romero to an outspoken espousal of the poor.

A month before his martyrdom, Grande also spoke of the shared table. "The material world is for all, regardless of national frontiers. What follows is therefore a common table, with celebratory table cloths for all, like this Eucharist."

Thought for the day

Jesus brought together at the same table those who had been separated for centuries – not because they had "earned" a place, but through God's goodness.

Prayer

Lord, as you did, so let us share our table with the despised of this world: refugees from Rwanda, people with AIDS, illegal immigrants, street children. We want to follow your example.

Amen.

Jon Sobrino
First week of Lent

First Sunday of Lent

God the liberator

Dt 26:4-10; Ps 90; Rm 10:8-13; Lk 4:1-13

"The Lord brought us out of Egypt . . ."

(Deuteronomy 26:8)

To Jesus, faith is belief in God who is Father, and availability to a Father who is God. Jesus rests in God the Father, but the Father is still God and does not let him rest.

We believers must likewise not rest; we must press on into the mystery of God; and to do this we have to go to the origin of his revelation.

At that origin, a liberating action took place: "He heard our voice and saw our oppression and brought us out of Egypt." At the beginning of God's revelation is compassion for a suffering people. God doesn't reveal himself to everyone in the same way, but shows himself to be on the side of the oppressed. This is not the God of the ancient European empires, nor the God of Christianity, nor the God of a "civil religion"; rather, this is the God of the poor.

God's revelation takes place through an action, liberation from slavery. Before worship comes the historical fact. The "option for the poor" and "liberation" are not Latin American discoveries of a few decades ago; they originate in God's revelation and belong to his deepest mystery.

The creed of the ancient Jews, like that of the New Testament, begins with an action of God, who liberates a victim. "God resurrected Jesus," said the first Christians.

Peter explains the action of God as if it were a two-act play. In the first act, Peter tells the Jewish people, "You murdered Jesus of Nazareth." It is the action of humankind that brings death and creates victims. In the second act, there is God's reaction to what humankind has done: "But God raised him from the dead."

The resurrection of Jesus has, then, the same structure as the liberation from Egypt. God dispenses justice to a victim and saves the oppressed from death. So resurrection should not be understood as the coming back to life of a corpse, but as the justice God gives to the crucified.

Faith in God means acting like God, being as good as our Heavenly Father, who liberates oppressed people, works justice and brings victims back to life.

Thought for the day

Let us remember the words of the leading Latin American theologian Gustavo Gutierrez: "God must be contemplated and practised."

Prayer

Father, help us to contemplate you, to let ourselves be loved by you. Then we will experience the grace which brings liberation.

Amen.

God's final word

Lv 19:1-2, 11-18; Ps 18:8-10; Mt 25:31-46

"I was hungry and you gave me food."

(Matthew 25:35)

Through the Old Testament prophets God says time and again: "I desire justice, not sacrifice." Jesus repeated this throughout his life. The words are absolutely clear; everyone understands them. They correspond to a deep human conviction, placed by God himself in our hearts: God wants us to abhor evil and do good.

Nevertheless, whether as human beings or as Churches, we invent a million ways not to see and do what is obvious. That is why this passage of the gospel according to Matthew is so important. It is a solemn teaching given at the end of Jesus' life, in which he states what will happen at the end of time. We are told how to live as human beings and as believers.

The gospel stresses that this is God's final word on the matter. There is nothing more to be said, by bishops or theologians, not even by Jesus himself.

Jesus says that everything is decided by "feeding the hungry": words which resound in the heart although their truth and beauty do not always set it on fire. There is nothing further. We cannot wriggle out of this statement. If someone asks where God is in all this, the answer is, "with the hungry". But we still cannot accept this and find a thousand ways to negate it in practice.

However, the Jesus of Matthew 25 must have been very present at the 1979 Latin American Catholic Bishops Conference in Puebla. This began by affirming the great truths of our faith: "Jesus Christ lives through his Church, principally in the Sacred Eucharist and in the proclamation of his word. He is present in those who gather in his name and in the form of his chosen pastors."

Then, more fundamentally and in more stirring language, the bishops continue: "Jesus Christ chose to identify most compassionately with the weak and the poor." The text does not say simply "to be" but "to identify". It does not simply say "with" but "most compassionately with". It could not be spelt out any clearer than that.

The poor and God converge in Christianity. What Jesus says to us is that God is in the poor. There we find him whether we know it or not. And we find him not only because that is his place but also because we go there with compassion, mercy, justice and love.

Thought for the day

The simple question, "What needs to be done?" and the outrageous truth that "God's place is with the poor", are the centre of our whole faith.

Prayer

May Jesus' compassionate exhortation to feed the poor set our hearts on fire.

Amen.

First Tuesday of Lent

Praying in reverse

Is 55:10-11; Ps 33:4-7, 16-19; Mt 6:7-15

"Our Father . . ."

(Matthew 6:9)

How often have we said the Lord's Prayer? Nowadays we may add "Our Mother" to bring tenderness and the feminine life-force into the mysterious reality of God. Either way, we have said this prayer so often that it has become rote. Perhaps we should inject new life into it by starting at the end. Let's try it.

Deliver us from evil. That is what we ask, Lord. But as there is so much evil, deliver us at least from the senselessness of cultural globalisation. Deliver us from egoism, from being cold-hearted, from involvement in injustice and death. Deliver us from the dehumanising power of entertainment.

Lead us not into temptation. Let us not fall into the temptation of giving up because the revolutions of the poor are not victorious; into the temptation of using power to control and manipulate instead of helping the poor to grow, and all of us to grow with them.

Forgive us, Lord. And if you allow us to correct you, forgive us not as we forgive but as you forgive, as you welcomed back your son who left home. And perhaps as we see you full of pity and compassion we will become free of the sin of despising the weak of this world.

Give us this day our daily bread. But do not begin with us, who eat three meals a day, but with the 1,300 million people who live in abject poverty. May all, not just a few, of the people of this world be able to take their lives for granted. And may we all share the same table and so find true joy.

May your will be done. We say it with fear and trembling, because that will is mysterious and unfathomable. Lord, why do you allow so much evil, so much aberration? But that will is also a joyful mystery, because you love life.

May your kingdom come. With globalisation the much-vaunted "end of history" has not arrived, as many would have us believe. Rather, an anti-kingdom has come. This is why we want to hear Jesus say: "The kingdom of God is at hand." We want to see signs of the kingdom – healings, the casting out of demons, the acceptance of outcasts, solidarity amongst people.

Hallowed be thy name. Many try to manipulate you. They invoke your name to bless war and outrage. Lord, they demonise your name. We want to describe you as you are: good, just and true.

Our Father and Our Mother. We say it at the end like a great cry for the utopia in which we can all be a human family, not just a species dominated by the most powerful. At Creation you made a commitment to that utopia, and you remind us of it for ever in your son Jesus.

Thought for the day

Let us not fall into the despair of thinking that utopia is no longer possible.

Prayer

Abba, Father, with your son Jesus we want to commit ourselves to building your kingdom on earth.

Amen.

First Wednesday of Lent

The sign of the cross

Jon 3:1-10; Ps 50:3-4, 12-13, 18-19; Lk 11:29-32

"This wicked generation asks for a sign."

(Luke 11:29)

We human beings are curious about important events and like to have signs which show their meaning. In Jesus' time the scribes and Pharisees were intrigued to know whether he was the Messiah and when the kingdom would come. Jesus worked no sign to satisfy this curiosity. But the Scriptures do encourage us to interpret the signs of the times, to look very carefully if we want to understand the truth of things.

Paul says that we see the wisdom of God in Christ crucified. A human being, destroyed, by our sins: that is the sign of God hidden amongst us.

Archbishop Oscar Romero, who was martyred in 1980, said the same thing when, speaking about the torture and massacres happening in his country, he compared the Salvadorean people to Yahweh's Suffering Servant. And Ignacio Ellacuria, one of the Jesuits who died at the hands of the Salvadorean army in 1989, wrote something similar during his first exile in Madrid.

Amongst the different signs which are always given, there is in every era one which is outstanding and in the light of which all the rest should be interpreted. This sign is always of people crucified, and it is found consistently throughout history. The crucified people are the historical continuation of Yahweh's Suffering Servant.

In his characteristic style Ellacuria said of the five hundredth anniversary of the "discovery" of Latin America: "First the Spanish and Portuguese and now the Americans have left its people like a crucified Christ."

This is the mystery of our faith. The great sign is the cross which rises over this world. It is a sign of incredible evil but also of incredible love, the love of Jesus and of thousands of martyrs. It is the mysterious sign of God, of his impotence before such evil but also his loving presence beside those who suffer.

Thought for the day

We need to look very carefully if we don't want to miss the most important things in life.

Prayer

May the crucified peoples of the world be a light to us, as the star was a light to the Magi. And by that light may we take the first step towards the truth about our world – God's truth.

Amen.

What can I do?

Est 14:1-7; Ps 137:1-3, 7-8; Mt 7:7-12

"Protect me, as I am alone and have no other protector but you."

(Esther 14:4)

These are the words of a defenceless woman. They are the words which millions of people repeat today. With these words let us continue our previous reflection upon people crucified, from the perspective of our own responsibility. It is fine that we ask God to do something (in fact a lot!) about the situation. But what about us? What should we do in a world which crucifies entire peoples?

In a very apposite Lenten meditation, Saint Ignatius asks us to meditate upon our sins with thanks that God has embraced us, but also with utter seriousness because sin is what killed his son. Here the martyred Jesuit Ignacio Ellacuria takes this intuition of Ignatius further by saying: "Sin is what crucifies our people."

Just as Saint Ignatius asks us to place ourselves before Christ crucified and ask ourselves three questions, so Ellacuria asks us to place ourselves before the crucified people and ask: "What did I do for this people to be so crucified; what can I do to end this crucifixion; what must I do to help this people rise again?"

Certainly we must devote ourselves wholeheartedly to the cause of the crucified people. Yet we should also ask what we may receive from them. If this question appears somewhat strange, then we have not understood the Suffering Servant, nor Christ on the cross.

The word of God tells us that the crucified peoples have been chosen to save us all. And it is so. They open our eyes to the truth about our world, because they are the product of our hands, and we understand what we are from what we produce. They can move us to conversion or, to put it another way, if they do not move us to conversion, then one might wonder what on earth could.

As the Latin American bishops said in their Puebla document, these people offer us, time and again, the evangelical values of simplicity, welcome, and receptivity to God. They offer us and themselves a great hope. They offer us faith in the mystery of God and of his great love – often expressed in martyrdom.

Given that we are in Lent, let us also remember that they offer us forgiveness. This really has occurred, at least in El Salvador. The poor have accepted and embraced those who for years have not only failed to defend them, but have co-operated with their oppressors.

Thought for the day

Let our aim this Lent be to bring the crucified peoples down from the cross and to open ourselves to all they have to give.

Prayer

Lord, let us not make the mistake of despising the oppressed people of the earth. Instead, give us too the nobility of heart to forgive those who wrong us.

Amen.

First Friday of Lent

A litany of madness

Ezk 18:21-28; Ps 129; Mt 5:20-26

"Be reconciled to your brother before leaving your offering at the altar."

(Matthew 5:24)

Jesus invites us to look at the world in a completely different way. It seems a strange, almost insane, message. It is not just a series of commandments, a set of rules. It is a call for a radical change of direction. If humanity does not make this change of course, it has no future.

First, we have to uphold our belief in a better world, in spite of everything that might make us lose hope. Only our faith in this alternative world – a world so unusual and yet so close – makes true life possible.

Next, we will require a kind of madness if we are to change the course of our world. The Gospel demands that we question everything, challenge everything, that we accept what the world rejects and do what the world thinks impossible.

To be fully human, we have to purify the air in which our spirit breathes. We have to "filter" the world around us, to create a cleaner, healthier environment. Our world needs a "spiritual ecology".

We can celebrate this as a litany challenging the values of the world and striving to create the values of the Gospel. It is a "litany of madness".

Let us challenge the spirit of individualism, and celebrate and promote the spirit of community.

Let us challenge racism and ethnocentrism, and celebrate openness and diversity.

Let us challenge lazy imitation, and promote inventiveness and creativity.

Let us challenge mere tolerance and indifference, and strive instead to create true understanding and compromise.

Let us challenge mere "good deeds" that leave the causes of suffering untouched, and strive instead to create a true spirit of justice.

Let us challenge complacency and self-sufficiency, and strive instead to build solidarity and interdependence.

Let us challenge propaganda and lies, and strive instead to build the spirit of truth.

Let us challenge what is hypocritical and self-righteous in the Church and strive to build a Church of the poor and the powerless.

Thought for the day

What Christianity offers seems like madness – to make this world's inhumanity become human.

Prayer

Lord, may our spirits breathe the pure air of your divine madness.

Amen

First Saturday of Lent

Walk humbly

Dt 29:16-19; Ps 119:1-2, 4-5, 7-8; Mt 5:43-48

Blessed are they who walk in the path of the Lord.

(Psalm 119:1)

To end this week's meditations, we have a psalm which speaks of "walking". We know it well. Our faith tells us that we come from a good beginning, that grace generated what we call life. In hope we walk towards a fullness where God will be all in all. But between these poles lies history: the way.

It is Jesus who shows us that the Christian religion is a religion of walking. It is expert in the process of walking forward through history.

This brings us to the familiar text of Micah (6:6-8). If we place it in a modern context, it seems as though God, with a mix of seriousness and humour, were saying to us: "Again you come to me with questions. Well, I shall speak to you for the last time and I shall be so clear that you will be left in no doubt." And the prophet says: "You have already been told what is good and what the Lord desires of you: merely that you practise justice, that you love tenderly and walk humbly with your God."

If we make a liberal translation of this text, we might conclude that we must announce the kingdom of God and transform the world, that is, practise justice. We must announce the good news, and be evangelists by loving tenderly. And all of this must be done as human creatures, walking humbly with God.

Thus, in the beautiful words of the martyred archbishop Oscar Romero, we may "have the joy of feeling ourselves accompanied by God throughout our history".

The German theologian Karl Rahner says that the more we carry the Gospel, the more it carries us. This is the ultimate Christian paradox: our life is a burden simultaneously heavy and light. We all know it is a heavy load, and Lent reminds us that our sins add to our burdens and those of others. But life can also be a light burden – blessed and full of hope.

The psalm reminds us that "blessed" is he who does God's will. Jesus often called "blessed" the poor, charitable, clean of heart, those who are hungry and thirsty for justice, those who are persecuted for the kingdom. And the Book of Revelation says: "Blessed are those who die in the Lord."

Thought for the day

Blessed is the one who, in history, walks humbly with God.

Prayer

Lord, we know that joy is possible. Help us to carry the Gospel, so that this possibility becomes a reality.

Amen.

Margaret Hebblethwaite
Second week of Lent

Second Sunday of Lent

A place to call home

Gn 15:5-12, 17-18; Ps 26; Ph 3:17-4:1; Lk 9:28-36

"I am the Lord," he said to him, "who brought you out of Ur of the Chaldeans to make you heir to this land." "My Lord, the Lord," Abram replied, "how am I to know that I shall inherit it?"

(Genesis 15:7-8)

We all want to be chosen, we all want to be loved, we all want to belong to a family, we all want to have a home. This Sunday's readings hover around these themes. The gospel gives the great announcement on the Mount of the Transfiguration that Jesus – despite the setback of his "passing" or death in Jerusalem – is nonetheless the chosen Son, the loved Son of God. Through his Sonship we are all drawn into becoming children and heirs of God.

The epistle promises us a homeland in heaven, such that no-one can ever take it away. We all need a home, a country, somewhere to live where we belong and where we can live without fear of eviction. Whatever our deprivations in this world, we are assured that in the eyes of God we are worthy of a wonderful home that we can call our own.

The Old Testament reading is about the promise of land as an inheritance. Without that inheritance, the promise of innumerable descendants would hardly be good news: to have a family and to be homeless is an agonising burden.

In many countries, people are at risk of death if they do not have land, because without a social security safety net they depend on a little plot of land for the opportunity to grow food. Sadly, in such countries the land is often in the hands of a small number of rich landowners, and a cycle of inheritance is set up in which the majority of the people never have a chance to break in on the pattern of ownership to provide for their families.

They are not asking for anything grand or privileged – even though as children of God they deserve the very best. They just want the chance to establish themselves enough to live in simplicity and to keep their children fed, clothed, healthy and housed.

God's promise to Abraham of inheriting land – and through him to all of us who belong to Abraham's spiritual family – is therefore crucially important. It is the promise of something that is an absolute necessity, and yet that so many people lack. That is why land reform is such a critical issue in so many poor countries, and why such a reform is an echo of the divine will for us as children and heirs of God.

Thought for the day

Every fiftieth year, in the Old Testament, there would be a jubilee, when land would be restored to those who had had to sell it because they were poor.

Prayer

God grant that every one of us may live in peace and unafraid, under our own vine and fig tree, or in our own modest home.

Amen.

Second Monday of Lent

False gods

Dn 9:4-10; Ps 78; Lk 6:36-8

"We have not listened to your servants the prophets, who spoke in your name to our kings, our princes, our ancestors, and to all the people of the land."

(Daniel 9:6)

Today's readings all follow the central Lenten theme of repentance for sin. The Old Testament reading comes from the book of Daniel, which is constantly exploring the theme of sin as it relates to political life, and particularly the way the kings were tempted to usurp the position of God.

The stories in Daniel are quite well known. King Nebuchadnezzar throws Shadrach, Meshach and Abednego into the fiery furnace because they refuse to worship a golden statue; but the angel of God walks through the flames with them and keeps them safe.

Then Nebuchadnezzar's son, King Belshazzar, throws a feast where a disembodied hand writes a mysterious message on the wall; Daniel is brought in to decipher it, and tells the king that the days of his kingdom are numbered because he has praised the gods of silver and gold, instead of honouring the true God.

A third famous story is that Daniel himself is thrown into the lions' den by the next king, Darius, because Daniel insisted on praying to God instead of idolatrously praying to the king; but the lions refused to eat Daniel so his life was saved. The passage that forms today's first reading is a prayer spoken by Daniel, in repentance for just such a national situation of idolatry.

Idolatry is a theme that seemed out of date for a long time, but the liberation theologians of Latin America find it very relevant to the false values that are influential in their countries today. In the little country of El Salvador, in the chapel of the University of Central America, there is a panel behind the altar that shows the great Archbishop Oscar Romero, like a sort of latter-day Daniel, pronouncing the unwelcome words of truth and justice in the face of symbols of idolatry – the power of weapons, the power of money, and a golden statue of an animal, with a clenched fist behind it. These represent the forces that have ruled in El Salvador.

Unlike Daniel, Archbishop Romero did not escape with his life after he challenged the repression meted out by the state. He was shot dead while saying Mass on 24 March 1980. His death calls us all to repent of the false gods in our lives – power, wealth, and the violent means that are sometimes used to preserve economic dominance.

Thought for the day

After the Titanic hit an iceberg and was on the point of capsizing, the band went on playing and the people went on dancing, oblivious to the coming disaster.

Prayer

God, grant that we may hear the words of today's prophets, and that our eyes may be open to see impending disasters before it is too late.

Amen.

Second Tuesday of Lent

Scarlet sins

Is 1:10, 16-20; Ps 49; Mt 23:1-12

"Cease to do evil.
Learn to do good,
search for justice,
help the oppressed,
be just to the orphan,
plead for the widow."

(Isaiah 1:16-17)

Orphans and widows are two very vulnerable groups – not much has changed since Isaiah spoke. Around the world today it is children and women who suffer the worst injustices.

Sex tourism is a pernicious industry, mostly affecting Asia, where children from poor families are robbed of their innocence to be turned into prostitutes for first world men. People justify it by saying "they are used to it", or "they are glad to do it for the money".

Street children are despised, persecuted and sometimes even shot dead in some Latin American countries. Deprived of their childhood, they develop a survival mentality that is used as an excuse for treating them as sub-human criminals.

In very many countries there are double standards for men and for women regarding sexual behaviour and obligations within marriage. A Tanzanian woman who shouted for help in the night when she found her husband raping her daughter was blamed because she had brought shame on her husband.

The custom, found in India, of paying expensive dowries makes women an economic liability and leads to the abortion or infanticide of innumerable girl babies. All around the world, women are often prevented from owning their own property, or managing their own money. There has even been a traditional custom of widows being expected to commit suicide on the death of their husbands.

Well may Isaiah speak of sins being "like scarlet": again and again we find that the worst sins draw blood. Yet today's promise is that even such blood stains can be wiped out and made "as white as snow". We may be reminded of the vivid image from the Book of Revelation of people who had "washed their robes white in the blood of the Lamb" (7:14).

The condition that God lays down for such cleansing is that we recognise human equality. Women and children may be vulnerable, but those with power and those with none must be treated with completely equal respect. As Jesus teaches us in today's gospel: we have only one Master, one Father, one Teacher, for all are sisters and brothers.

Thought for the day

A society is civilised in so far as it protects and brings freedom to its vulnerable members, especially women and children.

Prayer

God, give us the playfulness and humility of children, and the strength and gentleness of women.

Amen.

Second Wednesday of Lent

A price to be paid

Jr 18:18-20; Ps 30; Mt 20:17-28

"Anyone who wants to be great among you must be your servant, and anyone who wants to be first among you must be your slave, just as the Son of Man came not to be served but to serve, and to give his life as a ransom for many."

(Matthew 20:26-8)

It is easy enough for those in command to talk about their work being the service of others, but all too often we sense there is some duplicity in their approach. Do the bosses really take a lead in washing up the teacups and cleaning the loos? Or do they label their most unpopular actions as "service" to try to secure the compliance of their juniors and to add a holy veneer to a position of dominance?

St Ignatius of Loyola warned us how difficult it is to avoid self-deception in such areas. He told the story of some people who had acquired the sum of 10,000 ducats through slightly questionable means. They wished to be free of any inordinate attachment to this money, but wanted to become detached in such a way that they did not actually have to give it up. So, says Ignatius, "God is to approve what they themselves want."

Our first world attitude to the debt of the developing nations is often like that. We want the poor to be free from debt. We want the banks to let them off. But we do not want to carry the burden of the economic shortfall ourselves. There is always some other fictional fat cat who we think can afford these things – not ourselves.

Yet the whole of scripture is riddled with the theme of a painful reversal of fortunes. Kings are conquered, people are enslaved or sent into exile, shepherds are picked out for the highest favours, prisoners are set free. And in today's gospel we hear the same promise of a reversal of fortune: the greatest must become the slave.

Mary's Magnificat in Luke's gospel is the classic example of a change of fortunes, and it makes uncomfortable reading for anyone who is not marginalised or hungry. God has routed the self-satisfied, she says, overthrown those in positions of power, and sent the rich away empty. Meanwhile God has raised up those at the bottom of society and filled the hungry with good things.

We want those promises for the poor and hungry, but without ourselves falling into their former misery. But we are called to a greater generosity of spirit and a firmer trust, so that we are willing to go through poverty and hunger if that is God's will. In short we are called to drink the cup that Jesus drank.

Thought for the day

The service of God is perfect freedom.

Prayer

God, give me the strength to become a servant, and such a thirst for justice that I may drink the cup of your passion.

Amen.

Second Thursday of Lent

Open your eyes

Jr 17:5-10; Ps 1; Lk 16:19-31

"There was a rich man who used to dress in purple and fine linen and feast magnificently every day. And at his gate there lay a poor man called Lazarus, covered with sores, who longed to fill himself with the scraps that fell from the rich man's table."

(Luke 16:19-21)

The story of the rich man and Lazarus is well known to us, so it is tempting to think that we know it all. But if we dwell on familiar stories we can always find more in them.

One point that we may not have noticed is that the rich man does not refuse any direct request for help: we are never told that Lazarus asks for anything. This is not a beggar pestering for small change; not a charity mailing that gets thrown in the wastepaper basket; not a pressure group putting out an appeal on the radio or in the press. The rich man's sin is not that he says "no", but simply that he does not attend to what is staring him in the face. He is blamed because he lived with a juxtaposition of wealth and poverty and did nothing about it.

No one today can pretend they do not have a Lazarus lying at their gate: television and the press bring those juxtapositions of wealth and poverty into every home. Unless we all allow ourselves to notice and to do something, we will suffer the fate of the rich man – one of eternal regret.

I am reminded of the excuses made by some monks who lived close to a concentration camp during the Second World War. After the war they were asked why they had done nothing about the camp. They had been very busy, doing good works. They had not had time to ask questions about what was happening next door to them.

Again, a priest in Argentina was asked why he had done nothing about the prison in his parish: some 30,000 people disappeared during the dirty war in torture chambers such as were to be found inside that place. He did not know; he was too busy; he had not realised.

But Jesus tells us, "Blessed are your eyes because they see, your ears because they hear" (Matthew 13:16). Or, as the Old Testament reading for today puts it, "A blessing on the one who trusts in the Lord . . . like a tree by the waterside that thrusts its roots to the stream." But the one who trusts in human beings and fleshly or worldly comforts "is like dry scrub in the wastelands". Our true wealth, our true happiness, is found in loving our sisters and brothers in God.

Thought for the day

The Brazilian liberation theologian Clodovis Boff pointed out: "The life of a tree comes from the roots and not from the crown."

Prayer

God, open our eyes to what we are afraid to see, and our ears to what we are ashamed to hear. Give us that love that takes away our fear and shame.

Amen.

Second Friday of Lent

Not revenge but reconciliation

Gn 37:3-4, 12-13, 17-28; Ps 104; Mt 21:33-43, 45-6

"What do we gain by killing our brother and covering up his blood? Come, let us sell him to the Ishmaelites."

(Genesis 37:26-7)

It can sometimes happen, even to the best of people, that another human being causes them so much trouble that they wish they were dead. It can happen, for instance, to women who suffer violence from their partners. But there is no escaping the blood guilt, as Lady Macbeth found in her troubled sleepwalking. Even the death of a relative, let alone the killing of one, disturbs the survivors for longer than they could have believed possible, whether the relationship has been a good one or a bad one.

It is not surprising, then, that Reuben suggested his brother Joseph should not be murdered, but be disposed of in some other way. By selling him into slavery to some Ishmaelites travelling to Egypt, they thought they could safely count on never seeing him again. If they had thought there was any chance of him returning into their lives to haunt them for their evil act, they would probably have killed him instead.

As we know, Joseph did turn up in their lives again, when he had become the governor for the Pharaoh, and when his brothers unknowingly turned up in his court to seek food in a famine. The emotions at that meeting must have been unimaginably powerful: fear, shame and guilt on the side of the brothers; and on the side of Joseph the most amazing forgiveness. He wept so loudly with joy at finding his family "that all the Egyptians heard", and he assured his brothers: "Do not reproach yourselves for having sold me here, since God sent me before you to preserve your lives."

Joseph's forgiveness mirrors the mercy of God: Jesus told us that when we are sorry for our sins there is joy in heaven, not anger. It also mirrors the forgiveness that the poor and enslaved peoples of the world feel towards those who are oppressing them economically, by locking them into exploitative terms of trade in which the original producers receive almost nothing and the multi-national companies receive all the profit.

Thought for the day

The poor generally do not want revenge or to rub in the blame. They simply want the relationship to come right, so that everyone can be happy together.

Prayer

God, we are so ashamed at times of our greed and selfishness that we just want to justify ourselves instead of saying sorry. Let your forgiveness run ahead of our shame so that we are not afraid to enter a new relationship with you.

Amen.

Second Saturday of Lent

The wall can fall

Mi 7:14-15, 18-20; Ps 102; Lk 15:1-3, 11-32

As far as the east is from the west so far does he remove our sins.

(Psalm 102:12)

Anyone who has crossed the Atlantic knows it is a very long journey over a very big ocean. Even travelling at the fantastic speed of a jet plane, it takes hours and hours. And that is just from one part of the western world to another. The journey from east to west – say, from India to the Americas – is even longer.

Yet God removes our sins from us as far as the east is from the west. Or, as the first reading from Micah says, God throws all our sins to the bottom of the sea.

Removing our sins is not the same as excusing them. Removing them means getting rid of them totally, which means that we change. Our change of heart, or repentance – which happens by God's grace and in response to the prior offer of forgiveness – means that we really become different.

So being forgiven makes us happy, not just because it means God is not angry with us but because we become new people, different from the way we used to be. It is better than a new hairdo or a new set of clothes: we have a new spirit within us.

The gulf between east and west is not just a matter of geographical distance. It is also a matter of wealth. One fifth of the people in the world receive four fifths of the total world income; three fifths receive less than six per cent. The

358 richest people in the world own as much as the combined revenues of the countries where 1,300 million human beings are living without the basic necessities of life. In a world which could easily feed many more than its current population, 34,000 children die daily from malnutrition.

If removing sin means not just excusing sin but actually changing the situation so that the sin does not continue, then there is hope indeed. If God's promises are true, then this gross and obscene inequality can come to an end. We can live as a proper human family, where all the siblings care about each other and share the household's resources according to the needs of each. We can live in a world where justice and equality hold sway. Then the will of Our Father will indeed be done on earth as it is in heaven.

Thought for the day

No-one could have believed the speed with which the wall fell between eastern and western Europe, or the speed at which eastern and western Germany were reunited. Let us pray that the wall may also fall with speed between the east and the west of the world – or as many prefer to say, between the north and the south.

Prayer

God, give a new heart to your children, and put within us a new spirit, that the world may follow your laws and put into practice your principles.

Amen.

Thomas Cullinan
Third week of Lent

Third Sunday of Lent

The cry of the poor

Ex 3:1-8, 13-15; Ps 102; 1 Co 10:1-6, 10-12; Lk 13:1-9

God said to Moses, "I am aware of my people's sufferings . . .
Go and tell them: I AM has sent me to you."

(Exodus 3:7, 14)

Moses had grown up in the security of the royal household with all the blessings of a good education. He did not share the plight of his own people, his kith and kin.

But he awoke to their condition and, perhaps conscious of how he had compromised with the oppressive structures of sin, he over-reacted and had to flee from Egypt.

In due course he comes to Mount Sinai. It is the place of encounter with God. And God reveals himself as the one who has heard the cry of the poor. Not the one who has to be persuaded to listen but the one who heard the cry long before Moses even knew of it.

He is the God who will deliver his people in the face of all the power which Pharaoh will muster. He is the God who will bring his people through the painful processs of liberation into the land of promise and blessing.

Moses realises he is in the presence of his living God. But he can see that his own people are not going to take his new commission seriously. (Perhaps the jibe that sent him fleeing still rings in his ears: "Who made you prince and judge over us?")

God finds Moses' misgivings a reason for pressing on, not holding back. He gives him the assurance that I AM will be with them as I AM was with them in the past.

Moses has engaged, withdrawn, encountered God, and now re-engages. It is the pattern in the lives of all whom God uses to generate new life and new possibilities – certainly in the life of Jesus himself.

In the alternative gospel for today the Samaritan woman meets the one whose thirst precedes hers, and indeed reveals to her the true nature of her own thirst. The dialogue that follows reaches its supreme point when she is able to hear Jesus say, "I AM is the one who is speaking to you."

Lent is our (modest) time of withdrawal to let us encounter I AM – who heard the cry of the poor, who is speaking to us, and who sends us back to re-engage. The initiative is his, the obedience is ours.

Thought for the day

What steps are we taking to make sure that we engage and withdraw and re-engage?

Prayer

Holy Spirit, awaken us to know the compassion of God and to realise that he is always present to people's sufferings before we are.

Amen.

Third Monday of Lent

God's wider purposes

2 K 5:1-15; Ps 41; Lk 4:24-30

*O send forth your light and your truth; let these
be my guide.*

(Psalm 41:3)

A few years ago Naim Ateek, an Anglican priest from
Jerusalem, came to Liverpool to speak about Israel and
Palestine. During question time I said that one could really
sympathise with the hard-line Israelis if their actions were
based on the biblical emphasis of being a chosen people
given a promised land. How could they avoid being an élite?

Naim explained that this is a wrong understanding of God's
purpose in scripture. God does not call his people to be a
virtuous élite but to be a people who will live his justice
and be an instrument of his compassion. And the real test
of that is how the people treat the vulnerable and strangers.
To be a chosen people is to be more, not less, under the
judgement of God.

In Luke's gospel today it is worth remembering that
Nazareth was a small place where everyone knew everyone
and Jesus, after thirty years, was still only known as the
carpenter's son. Extraordinary!

He has been away, following the Baptist and then his own
ministry. He returns, the local boy made good? Fame for the
place at last?

But he goes to the synagogue and produces his jubilee
manifesto. Good news for the poor. A time of God's justice

and compassion which would do nothing to boost the chosen people's sense of being a virtuous élite but everything to call them to share in God's wider purposes.

It was the sort of prophetic word of truth which made and makes crucifying demands on people's self-esteem. Especially when it comes from within their own ranks.

I wonder how many of us have really made our own those words from the Second Vatican Council: "The joy and hope, the grief and anguish of people of our time, especially of those who are poor or afflicted in any way, are the joy and hope, the grief and anguish of the followers of Christ as well. Nothing that is genuinely human fails to find an echo in their hearts."

Thought for the day

How does our local parish carry, in its life and its liturgy, the joys and hopes, the griefs and anguish of people at large?

Prayer

Holy Spirit, free us from all our vested interests, even our mental and emotional ones, which stop us hearing the prophets of our day.

Amen.

Third Tuesday of Lent

Creative non-violence

Dn 3:25, 34-43; Ps 24; Mt 18:21-35

"Lord, do not disappoint us; treat us gently, as you yourself are gentle."

(Daniel 3:42)

Why does Jesus so often return to the importance of learning the art of forgiveness? Have we trivialised what he really meant – as when we say, "It's O.K., it didn't really matter," or "Let's forgive and forget"?

There is a story from the Desert Fathers which I have long cherished: Abba Anastasius had a complete Bible, for use in the community. One day a young man came to visit and when he left took the book with him. When the community assembled for evening prayer they found the book missing and realised what had happened. But Anastasius would not send after the young man "lest he be tempted to add the sin of perjury to that of theft".

The young man went to the local book dealer and said: I have this fine book, will you give me forty pounds for it? Leave it with me, said the dealer, it is a fine book but I must find out if it is worth that much. So he took the book to Anastasius and asked if it was really worth forty pounds. Anastasius looked at the book and verified that it was worth a good deal more.

The young man returned and the dealer said: yes you can have forty pounds; I took it to Abba Anastasius and he said it is worth at least that. Is that all he said? asked the young man. Yes, that was all. Well, said the young man, I don't want to sell it after all. And he hastened back to the abba, and begged him to take the book back. My son, replied Anastasius, I make you a present of it, go in peace. Peace? cried the young man, I'll never have peace on those terms. So he became a novice and stayed for the rest of his life.

Creative non-violence is the art of refusing to compound violence with violence, refusing to allow our injured self-image to pretend that our enemies are God's enemies. Non-violence will not demean others to prop up our own sense of virtue, as individuals, as communities or as nations. It is not a programme for wimpishness, nor for pretending injustice does not exist. But it knows that God's sun and rain and mercy are essential for all of us alike. In the end it would rather die for truth than kill for truth. Jesus died praying for those who had contrived his death.

Thought for the day

To whom, or on what occasions, are we most likely to react defensively rather than act creatively?

Prayer

Holy Spirit, you brought Jesus to the ultimate act of unilateral disarmament on the cross. Teach us to follow him.

Amen.

Third Wednesday of Lent

Red lights and religiosity

Dt 4:1, 5-9; Ps 147; Mt 5:17-19

"Do not forget what your eyes have seen, nor let it slip from your heart."

(Deuteronomy 4:9)

An Irish missionary priest was driving me through the streets of Rome, weaving his way through the hectic anarchy, when he suddenly said: "No-one in our countries back home should try to understand Canon Law until they have driven a small car through the streets of Rome. We think rules are for keeping. Italians ignore them unless they help life."

A year later I was being driven by a sister out of Liverpool one Sunday afternoon. I told her that story. At that moment we were stationary at red lights. There was not a car in sight in any direction. A look of great liberation came over her face as she engaged gear and we drove through the red lights!

Different nationalities have different approaches to the relation between law and freedom. They vary from Italian anarchy to Anglo-Saxon straight-laced obedience (maybe the source of many problems in the European Community!).

It was a problem from the earliest Christian period, with teachers such as Paul urging people to grow up into the freedom of the Spirit and not cling to the security of law-keeping. And others saying that Jesus came to fulfil or complete the law, not to do away with it.

Jesus himself seems to have been insistent that in calling people away from mere rule-keeping and towards a rediscovery of the heart of God's will and of the Torah, he was in fact calling them to a greater and deeper fidelity. He was not letting them off the hook.

In his Rule for Monks, St Benedict has a chapter on various ways in which they can pursue a true and wholesome humility. At the end he comments that such discipline will in due course bring one to a natural and easy freedom, so that one acts out of love and not out of fear, or duty, or guilt, or trying to prove oneself. And this is the work of God's Spirit in us, who sets us free from fear and "oughteries".

In trying to shape our lives in communion with the poor, the homeless, the dispossessed, it is easy to act out of guilt or justification-by-good-works. But perseverance and trust in God's initiative in our lives set us free to respond out of love. Where the Spirit is, there is freedom (2 Corinthians 3:17).

Thought for the day

In what ways do we expect too much, or fear too much, of institutions or laws?

Prayer

Spirit of our living God, give us a cheerful, adult and free love within us. May we love your law without being legalistic, and run freely in your ways without being childish.

Amen.

Third Thursday of Lent

The God of alternatives

Jr 7:23-28; Ps 94; Lk 11:14-23

"If it is by the finger of God that I cast out devils, know that the kingdom of God has overtaken you."

(Luke 11:20)

In the course of his life Jesus passed across a series of thresholds. Each was prepared for by his life beforehand. But each was also a break with what went before.

The first was his move from thirty stable years at Nazareth, through baptism and the desert, into an unstable life of preaching and healing.

The second was his decision to head for Jerusalem. His evangelical and demanding preaching had led to increased conflicts and his own perception of the real issues at stake had become more radical. Intimacy with his Father and his passionate love of people made it necessary to present himself at the heart of the nation, knowing full well that it would result in his being handed over by, and to, the powers that be.

His third threshold, prepared for by those first two, was his climactic journey through death into resurrected life.

Jesus, and Jeremiah before him, each lived at times when their people felt deeply threatened by a foreign power. Some hoped to survive by compromise, some by resistance, some by leaving the big issues aside and focusing on personal and domestic virtue. What nobody wanted was a prophet suggesting that God was giving them an opportunity to rediscover the wider issues of social justice and solidarity, to rediscover God as the giver of new life and alternatives, not simply as one there to secure their vested interests. People were loathe to discover themselves, through repentance, as the bearers of God's newness, rather than being the fearful and innocent victims of alien forces.

Jesus and Jeremiah both read the signs of their times quite differently from their contemporaries, and both were bound to be misunderstood. They were the enemy within. The prophets of doom. The disturbers of the peace. And each carried in himself the prophet's longing for his people: if only they could take hold of this moment of peace, but they could not.

As Jesus journeyed to Jerusalem he had a profound sense of time running out. No sitting on the fence. No standing aside. It was a time for decision. If you are not for me you are against me.

Where are the prophetic voices God is giving us today – as regards the power of God over the powers that be, as regards the cry of the poor, as regards planet Earth?

Thought for the day

In what ways do we fail to reshape our lives when prophets confront us – as regards widening gaps between rich and poor – as regards time running out for the environment?

Prayer

Holy Spirit, may we love truth in whatever way and through whomsoever you speak it to us. And may we ever respond within the realities of our own callings.

Amen.

Third Friday of Lent

False loves

Hos 14:2-10; Ps 80; Mk 12:28-34

"We will not say 'Our God!' to what our own hands have made."

(Hosea 14:3)

The panel of *Any Questions* is sometimes asked: which of the Ten Commandments do you find most difficult? And I always think: they really mean the last seven commandments, not the first three.

It is sad how the popular mind has reduced religion to do's and don'ts of moral behaviour. Because the heart of religion, as of the Ten Commandments, is these first three – to love God with all our faculties, to reject god-substitutes (idols) in all their forms, and not to do in God's name what is not truly of God (the tendency in all religion to make God justify our pursuits).

In today's gospel, Jesus replies to the scribe's question by bringing together two commandments familiar to them both: to love God and to love our neighbour as ourself. It is the only time in the gospels where Jesus speaks of a commandment to love God. That is not, as many claim, because for Jesus the two loves are so merged that the only way we can love God is in our neighbour.

It is rather because Jesus hated the idea of God as a distant spectator waiting for us to start by keeping commandments. For him it is all the other way around. Love springs from the heart of God. "As the Father has loved me, and I have loved you, so you love one another." It is a cascade down a hillside spreading out in a pool.

All our human loves are in need of redemption if they are to mature as sacraments of God's love and be truly life-giving. This is so of erotic love, of the ongoing love of friends, of the universal love focused on those whom the world deems worthless, and of that love we are called to by allegiance in a family, a community or the Church (a call to be adult enough to journey with sin as well as sanctity). All these forms of love are precarious, able to trap themselves in feel-good narcissism, incestuous chumminess or forms of idolatry. Without a context beyond and greater than themselves they are liable to any amount of self-justifying kiddology!

In the end the question is not about keeping commandments. Jesus got on quite well with "naughty" people. In the end the question is whether we give ourselves to God or to substitutes for God.

Thought for the day

Lent is a time for naming our idols and addictions: from close little domestic ones to big national ones. Crosswords, my car, my salary, my workaholism, the stock market, national security . . .

Prayer

Holy Spirit, fill us with your love that we may come to know and love God in all things, and to know and love all things in God.

Amen.

Third Saturday of Lent

The structures of sin

Hos 5:15-6:6; Ps 50; Lk 18:9-14

"What I want is love, not sacrifices, knowledge of God, not offerings."

(Hosea 6:6)

It is easy for us to misunderstand Jesus' story of the Pharisee and the tax-collector. In English the word Pharisee has taken on a pejorative meaning, that of hypocrite. But in Jesus' day it still simply meant a member of a strict religious group, and in this story Jesus is not pointing at hypocrisy. After all, the Pharisee in the Temple was only claiming to do what all of us are called to do in Lent: prayer, fasting and almsgiving. Any of us who is fasting twice a week and giving a tenth of our income this Lent is in a position to cast the first stone.

And perhaps we also misunderstand the other man, thinking that his confession and hunger for God's mercy were about the sort of personal or domestic sins we would mention in confession. It is more likely that what he was bringing to God was a terrible realisation that his entire livelihood, and that of his family, was based on collaborating with the occupying powers in collecting taxes with his own mark-up added on.

It is the sort of realisation that can hit people today, perhaps quite suddenly, that almost everything they buy or take for granted involves them in unjust structures of sin. The sandals I wear cost £10 and began life in a poor Spanish household where the workers were paid 20 pence an hour for the labour. The car I drive is part of the ever-increasing violation of our environment. The radio I listen to began life in a sweatshop.

St Luke places this story a page or two before his account of the tax-collector Zacchaeus and his remarkable determination to take what action he could in the face of his own injustice. Perhaps Luke knew that between our awakening realisation and our decisions to act (more or less) justly there is a terrible gap, a space for humble acknowledgement that we are in sin: we do not know what to do about it, and we rest upon the mercy of God.

One of the most efficient ways of avoiding that conversion journey is to go on repeating (to God and to ourselves) the list of own virtues, religious practice and moral superiority to others. The pharisee in us does not really need God at all, but is sure that God needs us.

Thought for the day

Is our main agenda to preserve a self-image of purity and virtue, or is it to abandon ourselves, with dirty hands and hearts, to the creative mercy of God?

Prayer

Lord, we pray for ourselves who live in security that we may not regard our good fortune as proof of our virtue, nor rest content to have our ease at the price of other people's tribulation. (Reinhold Niebuhr)

Amen.

Mary John Mananzan
Fourth week of Lent

Fourth Sunday of Lent

Inner freedom

Jos 5:9, 10-12; Ps 34:2-3, 4-5, 6-7; 2 Co 5:17-21; Lk 15:1-3, 11-32

"This fellow welcomes sinners and eats with them."

(Luke 15:2)

One of the most admirable traits of Jesus, which is not often reflected upon in spiritual books, is his inner freedom. He was so secure in himself and so single-minded in his fulfilment of God's will that he did not allow the expectations of Jewish society to pressurise him into conformity.

This is most apparent in his relationships with people. He seemed to have a predilection precisely for the people shunned by the religious leaders of his times. These latter were horrified by the way he mixed with such people. He ate with tax-collectors, chatted with adulterous women, forgave prostitutes, put up pagans as models of faith.

He neither kowtowed to the rich nor condescended to the poor. I wonder if we could say the same thing about ourselves. If we are honest, we have to admit that we are often so awed by the wealthy, the famous and the powerful that we give them preference, we cultivate their acquaintance and make decisions in their favour. We want to bask in their reflected glory. There are few people who can treat the rich and poor with equal respect.

We talk so much about the option for the poor and solidarity with the poor, but how much do we really live these things out? Our actions are often tinged with pity and condescension. Sometimes we even react with impatience at the importunity of the poor.

"This fellow welcomes sinners and eats with them," the gospel tells us. Towards sinners Jesus did not display a judgemental, self-righteous attitude. He did not seem even to be motivated by a desire to convert them. He ate with them. He related to them on a social level. He shared their food. He actually enjoyed their company!

How different this is from the attitude of "good" people who honestly think that they should not be seen with someone who is "living in sin", because it might be misinterpreted as condoning their behaviour. Or from very zealous people who make it their objective to "bring back" their erring friends. They succeed only in alienating these people, who refuse to become objects of their reforming zeal.

We need to shed our attitudes of self-righteousness so that we can encounter people with profound respect. Our commitment to the poor must spring from genuine compassion rather than from condescending pity.

Thought for the day

Let us not seek to reform people. Let us be like Jesus and just love them.

Prayer

Jesus, I truly admire your inner freedom. Help me to discover the blocks and internal slaveries in me that hinder the development of this inner freedom.

Amen.

Fourth Monday of Lent

God is no kill-joy

Is 65:17-21; Ps 30:2, 4, 5-6, 11-13; Jn 4:43-54

*"There shall always be rejoicing and happiness in
what I create."*

(Isaiah 65:18)

This reading from the prophet Isaiah perfectly expresses the
joyful spirit of Laetare Sunday. It captures the mood even
better, perhaps, than the liturgy for that day.

Isaiah speaks of the creation of a new heaven and a new
earth. Jerusalem is to be a joy and its people a delight. God
will rejoice over the city and celebrate being with its people.

As we know, Jerusalem is a symbol of the Church, the
people to whom Christ has preached the Good News of
salvation. It is the Church which is to be full of rejoicing. We
are the people in whom God delights.

Christianity is certainly supposed to be Good News. But
sometimes I feel that for many people it has become a
burden – a preoccupation with what is forbidden and what
is allowed, what is sin and what is not sin. The legacy of
such a depressing kind of religion is guilt.

There is also a notion that sanctity must be a constant
dragging along of one's cross, a preoccupation with
suffering. Cold asceticism all too easily pushes out joyful
celebration. Why this joylessness in our Christianity? It is
as if we had a sadistic God who cannot stand it when we are
happy. As if this kill-joy God had to send us suffering to
make us holy.

That is why my heart lifts when I come across today's reading from Isaiah: "There shall always be rejoicing and happiness in what I create." Believe it or not, God truly wants us to be happy, already here on earth and not only in the hereafter.

How could a God, who has made such a beautiful world and filled it with things for us to enjoy, desire us to be miserable? If God takes such pleasure in what he has made, cannot we do the same?

Isaiah's words remind me of Nataraz, the Hindu dancing God. Can you not imagine God dancing through heaven and earth and rejoicing in it, exclaiming with delight: "And it was very good!"

Thought for the day

We can choose to live Christianity as a daily dragging of our cross. But we can also dance with playful consciousness of God and his Creation.

Prayer

Creator God, you truly want us to be happy, to rejoice always. Infect us with your joy. Let this joy abide in us even amidst suffering. Let it buoy us up when we are weighed down by burdens we create for ourselves. Maybe when we are truly happy we will cease to destroy your Creation.

Amen.

The water of life

Ezk 47:1-9, 12; Ps 45; Jn 5:1-3, 5-16

"Come to the waters, all who thirst: though you have no money, come and drink with joy."

(Isaiah 55:1)

This entrance antiphon for today's Mass contains the theme of the readings: water. It is not only in the desert land of the Near East that water is all-important. It is important all over the world.

With today's ecological crisis, some political scientists predict that the conflicts in the next millennium will be mainly over water. We can see this already in the sad disputes between Jews and Palestinians over water supplies.

Water is indeed a precious commodity. It is more precious to life than diamonds, because we can live without diamonds, but we cannot live without water.

In the spiritual realm, water symbolises God's saving grace. God gives this grace to his people in great abundance, as pictured in the first reading from Ezekiel: "Wherever the river flows, every sort of living creature that can multiply shall live, and there shall be abundant fish; for wherever this river comes, the sea shall be made fresh. Along both banks of the river, fruit trees of every kind shall grow; their leaves shall not fade, nor their fruit fail." The responsorial psalm also talks of the river "whose streams gladden the city of God".

The images are so beautiful that it seems as if the Bible cannot let them go. They rise up again right at the end, in the

Book of Revelation. Once again we can bathe our feet in "the river of life, rising from the throne of God and of the lamb, and flowing crystal-clear". Once more we can taste of "the trees of life, which bear twelve crops of fruit in a year".

Is it any surprise that Jesus applied this lovely picture of water to himself? "Let anyone who is thirsty come to me," he cried out. "As Scripture says, from his heart shall flow streams of living water." How perfectly his words were fulfilled when, on the cross, water poured from his own body. In today's gospel, we are still by the healing water, as our reading shows the power of God to cure the sick in the Sheep Pool of Bethesda.

What we must remember is that this water, this source of life, energy and joy, is actually within each of us. Christ says when talking to the Samaritan woman that the water he will give will become in us a spring gushing up to eternal life.

Thought for the day

Do we truly believe that within each one of us there is an inexhaustible source of power, of joy and of life? If we do, we will not look for happiness outside of ourselves. No one – man or woman – can truly make us happy, because the source of true bliss is within us.

Prayer

Jesus, give us that water that you spoke of to the Samaritan woman. Give it especially to those "who have no money" – the poor and the marginalised. Water the parched earth of those who no longer see clearly the vision of the alternative society they have worked for all their lives. Plant in them the seeds of new hope.

Amen.

Fourth Wednesday of Lent

You are gods

Is 49:8-15; Ps 145:8-9, 13-14, 17-18; Jn 5:17-30

The reason why the Jews were even more determined to kill him was that he was not only breaking the Sabbath, but worse still was speaking of God as his own Father, thereby making himself God's equal.

(John 5:18)

As we go deeper into the Lenten Season, it is good to reflect on the reasons why the Jews condemned Jesus. The gospel gives us two: first, that he broke the Sabbath, and second that he made himself equal to God.

It has always intrigued me when I read again and again that Jesus performed healing on the Sabbath, going against the Jews' interpretation of the Law. I don't think Jesus did this just to provoke them. He wanted to make a point: that the Sabbath is made for human beings, not human beings for the Sabbath. And he illustrated this clearly by his healings.

Law is made for human beings, not human beings for the Law. Law has the peculiar characteristic that, as soon as it is made, it seems to assume an existence of its own. It is as though it is independent of human beings, so that even when it becomes oppressive, people seem helpless to change what they themselves have made.

Law, rules, and regulations are there to facilitate life and not to make it miserable. Self-righteous, legalistic people are the ones who make law a burden. What incensed Jesus about such people was not just the way they tied together great bundles of rules; worse was the fact that they would not help others to carry these bundles.

There are two wrong attitudes towards law: trying to get around it and blindly conforming to it. A lot of people think it is all right to do things against the law as long as one is not caught. Other people think that being good just means conforming to the law. But maybe the best attitude is responsible decision-making. It is a characteristic of Christ's inner freedom that he has a healthy respect for the law but does not allow it to become oppressive.

The second accusation against Christ is that he made himself equal to God. My reflection on this is that Christ had a gradual realisation of his divinity. And this is a legacy he left us: we too can gradually realise the divine in us.

This is actually the most important thing we have to accomplish in life. Such is the insight of all mystics, whether Christian, Hindu, Buddhist or Moslem. As the German mystic Meister Eckhart paraphrased it: "God became a human being so that human beings could become gods."

Thought for the day

Let us allow laws and rules to guide us. But let us in the end do what we think is right, and accept the consequences of our actions.

Prayer

God, let me discover you in the depth of my own being.

Amen.

Fourth Thursday of Lent

Idols

Ex 32:7-14; Ps 106:19-20, 21-22, 23; Jn 5:31-47

"They have cut for themselves an image of a calf and have worshipped it and sacrificed to it."

(Exodus 32:8)

The readings of this Mass help us to reflect in different ways on the same thing: the worship of the true God. The entrance antiphon exhorts us to "seek always the face of God", "to search for the Lord", which means to distinguish him from the idols we meet on the way. The first reading and the responsorial psalm talk of the molten image that the people of Israel created for themselves. And in the gospel, Jesus presents his credentials as the one truly sent by God.

Idolatry is a great temptation for the human race and for individuals. It has been down the ages and it still is today. Even those who reject religion very soon make a god for themselves.

Institutional religions themselves, which are supposed to be the mediators of God, sometimes present an image of God that is more of an idol. This idol obscures the true God who brings us joy. The images of God which we ourselves had as children can also be idols, and we need to shake ourselves free of their tyranny.

We are sometimes presented with a God who seems to take pleasure in making us suffer. The preoccupation of Christians, especially many Catholics, with sin and guilt comes from an image of God as a stern judge who is just watching until he catches you committing a sin and cannot wait to plunge you into hell.

Another idolatrous image of God is that of the warrior who leads his people to embark on religious wars in his name. How many innocent victims have been sacrificed to this false god!

Many of us have positive idols, but they are idols just the same. Positive idols are people to whom we are so attached that we no longer have a judgement or an opinion apart from theirs. A person on whom we are emotionally dependent is also an idol. Perhaps this is why a lot of battered wives go back again and again to their husbands, even though they may be economically independent.

Negative idols are people whom we allow to make us wilt, or the anonymous "they" who stop us acting on something because we are worried that they might disapprove, might start thinking badly of us or calling us names.

Thought for the day

We should make a declaration of independence from our idols, beginning with our idolatrous images of God and the super-egos that have run our lives for so long.

Prayer

Creative spirit, I sit in contemplation of your faceless presence. Do not allow me to make an idol of you, creating you to my own image and likeness. Detach me from all the positive and negative idols in my life.

Amen.

Fourth Friday of Lent

The cost of prophecy

Ws 2:1, 12-22; Ps 34:17-18, 19-20, 21, 23; Jn 7:1-2, 10, 25-30

The Lord is near to the brokenhearted and saves the crushed in spirit.

(Psalm 34:18)

The readings of this Mass focus on the sufferings of the just one. The first reading, from the Book of Wisdom, shows how the wicked plot against the just one because his very existence is a reproach to their evil ways. The gospel shows how the Jews were plotting the capture of Jesus, that awkward prophet who championed the rights of widows and affirmed the dignity of outcasts. The respectable and wealthy leaders are looking for a chance to kill him.

Between these two readings comes the psalm, with its assurance from God that the just one will not be abandoned: "The Lord is near to the brokenhearted, and saves the crushed in spirit."

It is the common experience of those who have committed themselves to justice and to the struggle of the poor and the oppressed that they become objects of persecution by those whose interests are endangered.

I am not like the great prophets of the past or the martyrs of the present. But in my own life, I do have opportunities to denounce injustice and to take up the cause of the oppressed; I have experienced being looked upon with suspicion, being labelled as subversive and radical, I have been accused of "agitation for rebellion" just because I opposed the rise in oil prices. But I haven't suffered like many Christians of our day.

I think of Ira Ford and the other Sisters who were raped and murdered in Salvador because of their solidarity with the poor. Then there were the Jesuits who were murdered on their campus in El Salvador for monitoring the abuses of human rights; and the white South Africans injured by parcel bombs because they spoke out against the evil of apartheid; and John Bradburne, the director of a colony of lepers in Zimbabwe who was gunned down when he stood up for their right to land.

In my own country of the Philippines I think of the many who suffered under the Marcos regime, the thousands who died through military action, who were tortured, raped, arrested in the middle of the night, imprisoned, put in isolation. I weep for them but I am also inspired by them, because it is truly admirable that men and women could give up comfort, security, and even their lives to make a better world for their people.

I would like to believe that these brave people experienced God's nearness in those moments when their spirits were crushed and their bodies mangled.

Thought for the day

There is a need for prophets at all times. Prophecy means not only announcing the good news but denouncing the bad news. That is why prophets are never crowned, rather many of them are beheaded. But amidst their sufferings God must surely give them consolation and joy that surpass our human understanding.

Prayer

Dear God, help me to be faithful in my commitment to justice, knowing that you are near those who are brokenhearted and you save the crushed in spirit.

Amen.

Fourth Saturday of Lent

From victims to survivors

Jr 11:18-20; Ps 7:2-3, 9-10, 11-12; Jn 7:40-53

O Lord my God, I take refuge in you.

(Psalm 7:1)

Each of today's readings is about innocent victims. The prophet Jeremiah says that he is "like a trustful lamb being led to the slaughterhouse". King David, in the responsorial psalm, laments that he is being hunted down even though there is no injustice on his hands. And in the gospel Jesus himself, the guiltless one, is under threat of arrest from the scheming Pharisees.

All of these innocent victims need a place of safety. Each of them could say: "O Lord my God, I take refuge in you."

I would like to reflect on this verse from the perspective of women who are victims of violence. We all know of the existence of shelters for battered wives and refuges for victims of rape and incest. But in many parts of the world there are not enough of them for the many victims of violence.

This is what really amazes me. In spite of all our efforts for the cause of women, the number of cases of violence against women has not actually gone down. It may even have risen. Violence against women cuts across class, race, nationality and creed. As a woman I am anguished at this continuing victimisation of women on a global scale.

A large proportion of the violence in the world today happens in the home. The perpetrators of violence and abuse include husbands, brothers-in-law, uncles, even grandfathers. It is almost unbelievable how people a child trusts can misuse them in such a way as to ruin their whole life. And if women and children are not safe in their homes, where can they be safe? Home is supposed to be a haven of security.

In the midst of such hopeless suffering and insecurity God offers a refuge. But God has no arms. When I was studying in Germany, there was a church I used to visit – the Ludgerikirche – that had a statue of Christ on the cross which had no arms: they were blown off when the church was bombed during the Second World War. Beneath the cross is written: "I have no arms, you are my arms."

Thought for the day

It is not enough for us to tell victims of violence that God offers them security and refuge. After all, God has no arms. We have to be God's arms and offer security and refuge to women and children who are victims of violence.

Prayer

God, look upon all the women and children all over the world who are victims of violence. Heal them with your love. Gather them to your heart. Help them not only to be healed but to transcend their victimhood to become survivors, wounded healers and agents of social transformation.

Amen.

Fifth week of Lent
Joan Chittister

Fifth Sunday of Lent

The living dead

Is 43:16-21; Ps 125; Ph 3:8-14; Jn 8:1-11

"Unbind him, let him go free."

(John 11:44)

It happened in Chiapas. I was sitting in a Zapatista camp surrounded by indians disguised by bandanas and holding rifles which they had told the entire country they did not want to use.

"What do you want and why are you doing this?" we asked them about this "revolution" that was more a plea for participation than a coup. "We want to be treated like human beings," they said. "And we are doing it because when we read the Gospel we learned that we *were* human. We want you to tell your people our story so that they will help us take our case to the Mexican government."

"Who, me?" I thought. And then I remembered today's gospel.

The interesting thing about the Lazarus story is that although Jesus calls Lazarus forth from his tomb, Jesus himself does not do the freeing of his friend. Jesus says to the gathered crowd, "Unbind him, let him go free."

The unbinding of those seeking to rise from the dead is left, in other words, to us. Jesus calls them to life but it is we who are left to unbind whatever burial clothes still smother them.

All over the world today, the poor are discovering that they too are human. They hear the call of Jesus to come forth from their graves of squalor, of degradation, of ignorance and of indignity into the kind of humanity that gives glory to God.

They want what we want: they want food, jobs and medicine for their young people, wages for their workers, homes for their families, education for their children. They want humanity. Is that too much to ask? And what does that cry for humanity have to do with our cry for spirituality?

It is so easy to say that Lent is a time of spiritual rejuvenation. But when almost two-thirds of the people of the world suffer a living death, what kind of spirituality is it that can wear ashes but never give alms, pray for God's favour for ourselves but shower none of it on others, provide welfare for the rich and little for the poor, insist that the poor work but hire them only part-time or refuse to provide the benefits that would give them security. What kind of spirituality is it that legislates for the suffering of others in the name of economic development and calls it justice?

Thought for the day

The spirituality of justice demands that I give myself to the unbinding of the poor who come forth seeking life.

Prayer

Loving God, give me a heart that hears your call to unbind the living dead and give them life.

Amen.

Fifth Monday of Lent

Count me out

Dn 13:1-9, 15-17, 19-30, 33-62; Ps 22; Jn 8:1-11

God heard her cry and, as she was being led away to die, he roused the holy spirit residing in a young boy named Daniel who began to shout, "I am innocent of this woman's death!" At which all the people turned to him and asked, "What do you mean by these words?" Standing in the middle of the crowd, he replied, "Are you so stupid, sons of Israel, as to condemn a daughter of Israel unheard, and without troubling to find out the truth?"

(Daniel 13:44-48)

Lent itself can be a temptation. It is so easy to turn our attention to ourselves, to make the "interior" life a place apart from the world around us, to turn religion into some kind of spiritual jacuzzi designed to soothe our hearts and remove from our shoulders the burden of co-creation.

But seductive as the message is, it is also deceptive. To the contemplative, the one who comes to see the world as God sees the world, Lent is the time when we renew our commitment to turn from the sins of the system around us in order to take our part in building the Reign of God. Teresa of Avila was very plain about the connection: "The purpose of prayer, my daughters," she said over and over again, "is good works, good works, good works."

The notion that the spiritual life is a private domain of the personally pious but publically unaware makes a mockery of the scriptures. Today's reading, in fact, dashes the very thought of such a thing. Here, a powerless woman and a young boy – neither one of them fully-fledged participants in the patriarchal system – confront that system with a question that rocks it to its knees, forces it back on itself, cries to heaven for response.

"I am innocent of this woman's death," the boy shouts. The meaning is clear: "I will not be part of such a thing," the boy cries out in the face of custom, in the face of system, in the face of those whose piety is righteousness rather than love. "I will not agree to the oppression," the woman says.

The implications for the rest of us are compelling. Lent – that time when we ask ourselves what it is we are really doing with our lives, what we are really giving ourselves to creating, what we are really modelling for the world – confronts us with this story that brooks no excuse of powerlessness.

Whoever we are, whatever we do, however we live, each of us can pull back from situations we are being drawn into and say "I am innocent of this. I do not agree with this thing we are doing in the office, at the party, in the church."

Each of us can pledge the conversion of our own heart and muster the courage to say so in order that the world around us may stop and reflect on what they are doing. Then Lent would be real and conversion would be possible.

Thought for the day

To plead powerlessness in the face of injustice is to be guilty of the oppression ourselves, whatever our own good intentions.

Prayer

God of justice, give us the grace to cry out against injustice whatever the cost, whatever the consequences to ourselves.

Amen.

Fifth Tuesday of Lent

Pay attention

Nb 21:4-9; Ps 101; Jn 8:21-30

God will turn to hear the prayers of the helpless;
God will not despise their prayers . . .
God looked down from heaven to the earth
to hear the groans of the prisoners
and free those condemned to die.

(Psalm 101:18, 20-21)

Lent is not about guilt. Lent is about awareness. It is amazing how easy it is to go through life and never notice what is going on around us, never wonder what God demands of us now, never pause to assess the present.

We simply go on from day to busy day, wishing for spiritual consolation and missing the great spiritual challenge that confronts us in the suffering of the world. We concentrate solely on our own problems, and we have learned to take the unconscionable for granted. We immerse ourselves so much in the daily, so routinely in the mundane, that we fail to see the call to the sacred in what needs to be changed in life as well as what needs to be praised.

Lent calls us to be aware of what is happening to our spiritual lives as a result. Lent requires us to pay conscious attention to more than our business lives and our social lives. In this day and age, the three facets of life – the spiritual, the economic and the social – are more separate than at any other time in history. We are private people now.

So, Lent calls us back to that place in ourselves where conscience dwells, where God is active in us, where we set ourselves to see the world through the eyes of God.

Today's readings are about the spiritual consequences of spiritual bondage: my own and everybody else's. When the world is in bondage to poverty, how can I possibly call my spiritual life complete until I lift a hand to change it?

Lent asks us what we see now in a world where welfare programmes in the richest countries of the world are designed to punish the children of the poor, where education is no longer an economic priority, where undemocratic debts crush the peasants of the world and where a new kind of industrial slavery hires only part-time workers or gives full-time workers around the world part-time pay. Lent reminds us that we are part of a people of God in a sinful world that waits for us to repent.

The question that Lent grinds into our soul is, where is my personal spiritual life in the midst of all that? How can I possibly think that I am following Jesus if I do not routinely take on the pain around me?

Thought for the day

Lent does not call us to wallow in past guilt. Lent calls us to be aware of Christ's call to us now to do our part in bringing about the reign of God on earth.

Prayer

Great God, give me a heart for the poor so that I may come to new awareness of your hurting presence here on earth and be always ready to respond.

Amen.

Fifth Wednesday of Lent

The furnace which purifies

Dn 3:14-20, 24-25, 28; Dn 3:52-56; Jn 8:31-42

"If our God, the one we serve, is able to save us from the burning fiery furnace and from your power, O King, we will be saved; and even if not, then you must know, O King, that we will not serve your god or worship the statue you have erected."

(Daniel 3:15-18)

The truth of this reading is perennial. It never changes. It always challenges. It touches everyone, everywhere.

The point of the reading brings us to new consciousness in life: if we refuse to worship what society says we must – if we refuse to bow down to the gods of this society, to consumerism, to ethnic chauvinism, to the domination of humans over the rest of creation, to sexism in the name of Church and family, and violence in the name of science and defence – we will get thrown into one social furnace after another. We will get called unpatriotic, or radical feminists, or heretics, or ecology freaks.

The rejection is not easy. There are many who know in their hearts that the profit and plunder of the age, the exploitation of peoples and the oppression of minorities is wrong.

What is difficult is saying so in the face of a system fattened on talk of "rugged individualism" and "initiative" and the need – in the wealthiest countries in the world – to "balance the budget" on the backs of mothers and children while we decry welfare for the poor and insist on the tax reductions and repatriation of profits that constitute our welfare programmes for the rich.

Lent is about summoning the courage it takes to walk the way of the cross with those being crucified today, whatever the cost to our own social status because of it.

What's more, as the Book of Daniel makes obvious, there is indeed no guarantee that God will save us from the pressures of such marginalisation, such scorn, such social ostracism. But that is not what is important.

What matters is that we do what we must to witness to the God who created this world to be kept and not plundered, who created women and men as equals and not one the servant of the other, who told Peter to put away his sword despite the best of causes, who built a community on love and not on lordship.

Then, God will walk with us and God will hold us up and God will bless the heart that is purified of rust and dross, of narcissism and domination, of self-centredness and pathological individualism. Then, we will find the strength to be what we must be.

Thought for the day

To worship anything less than God is to dwarf our own souls and to deny ourselves the right to be living flames.

Prayer

God of life, give us the grace to risk our own existences so that all of life may become what it is meant to be.

Amen.

Fifth Thursday of Lent

Remember these marvels

Gn 17:3-9; Ps 104; Jn 8:51-59

Consider our God and God's strength;
constantly seek this face.
Remember the wonders God has done,
the miracles, the judgements God spoke.

(Psalm 104:4-5)

It is very easy in the midst of personal pressures and private confusions, of public stress and social challenge, to forget the wonders God has done for us. God often performs these marvels when we are least hopeful they will happen, least sure they can happen.

Out of death, after pain diminishes and numbness fades, new life so often comes forth. After the loss of one direction, another more vibrant than the first so often emerges. Beyond what the world says are our best years, comes a fullness of life unmatched by any other stage.

These are the miracles of life. These are the wonders we stumble into, so obviously not of our own making that they must be of God. These are the things that must be remembered in the midst of the daily, dull, depressing moments of life.

Good has so often come out of even the more shabby parts of our own life. We retreat from religion because it disappoints, only to find no better answers elsewhere and return more spiritual than ever before. We fail ourselves miserably, then find new life when we discover that people loved us for ourselves, not our images. We get stopped in our indulgent, dishonest, ambitious, shiftless tracks and become newer, better selves. These are the wonders of life.

It is a wholesome part of Lent, then, to remember where God has been faithful and we have strayed, how God has loved us even when we have been least lovable, least aware, least immersed in the mind of God. We need to rehearse in our hearts that it was often in darkness that God was clearest to us. For without memory, hope dies.

The creation of the Covenant did not end the struggles Israel had to face. It simply confirmed the fact that whatever fray they faced, they would not be alone.

Our own lives take the same pattern yet. Every life is filled with a series of small miracles designed to carry us through dark days, up steep mountains, down into the valley of death, beyond every boundary.

One of the spiritual disciplines of Lent is to recognise these, to let praise rise in our hearts. We need to see the miracles of our lives as signs along the way that no path is too twisted, no burden so heavy, no social system so impenetrable as to confound us utterly. The God who has sustained us in the past will not desert us in the present.

Praise and memory take us into tomorrow with open minds and certain hearts.

Thought for the day

Those who forget the blessings of their lives have no strength for the future.

Prayer

Loving God, give us the grace to remember the miracles of life, to praise you for them and to take them as promise in the face of uncertainty.

Amen.

Fifth Friday of Lent

Patriarchs and prophets

Jr 20:10-13; Ps 17; Jn 10:31-42

Sing to the Lord, praise God who has delivered the souls of the needy from the hands of the evil ones.

(Jeremiah 20:13)

Both Jeremiah and Jesus incur the enmity of those who stand to lose most from the power of their challenges and the constancy of their irrepressible cry for goodness where only public sham prevailed.

Friends who did not want their lives to change as the prophet Jeremiah demands shunned him. Conservatives who preferred the letter of the law to the vision of new life that Jesus presented hounded him down. "The souls of the needy" were not their determining priority. They wanted things as things had always been, yes, but they wanted more than that. It was not simply the faith they were defending; it was the system that supported their status to which they were really committed. It was themselves, not their God, they were protecting.

It is the keepers of the status quo who demand always that the preservation of the system be put above the laws of creation and the love of God. Every system seeks to preserve itself at all times and, as often as not, in the name of God and goodness.

It is a seductive argument. We preserve the businesses of the rich before we preserve the houses of the poor because "God helps those who help themselves". We preserve the military before we preserve schools because we stand "for God and country". We preserve the privileges of the men of the world and never even ask if women have any rights as well because that is "God's will for women". The system saves itself at all times, whatever the prophetic word of God.

Lent, on the other hand, requires us to see sin where sin is, to see the sins behind systems that oppress, to listen to the Word that brings the Jesus who came that we might all have life – and have it more abundantly. Why?

Because, in the end, God will work God's will and what, deep down, our hearts have always known to be right our eyes will see to be true. That is called, in fact, "the reign of God".

The only question then will not be how many Masses we attended in our lifetime, how many private penances we did every Lent, how close we came to fulfilling the institutional checklist of dogmas and doctrines. It will be how many times we put the Word above the system and the Gospel before the Law, whoever rejected us, whatever it cost.

Thought for the day

Lent is really about honouring the prophetic word rather than the systemic word.

Prayer

God of justice and of love, give us the grace to live your Word in the face of systems more intent on preserving themselves than on converting themselves.

Amen.

Fifth Saturday of Lent

Room to roam

Ezk 37:21-28; Jr 31:10-18; Jn 11:45-56

Yahweh will guard us as a shepherd guards the flock.

(Jeremiah 31:10)

Lent is not about failure. Lent is about conversion.

The image of God as shepherd makes for an interesting insight into the process and the meaning of spiritual growth. The fact is that shepherds follow flocks as much as they lead them. Shepherds give sheep a great deal of latitude on the hills. They allow the flock to mix with other sheep; they watch them at lonely distances as they climb to great and solitary heights, they allow them to poke and gambol along at their own rates of speed. They trust them and give them range to roam in search of the grasses they need for nourishment.

But then in the end, if one is lost, the shepherd drops everything to find and carry it back to the fold.

Lent reminds us not only of our failures, but of our excursions into growth along the way, of what we have discovered from our goings and comings, of what we have learned about the price to be paid for the roads that we have taken.

Lent brings to mind the range of our own roaming, it makes us assess the heights to which we've climbed, the risks that we've taken, the expense of the journey in energy and gain, and the value of the growth for which we have expended ourselves.

It reminds us, too, of the number of times we have been too weary, too spent, too confused to find our way alone and have been brought back by the grace of God from the brink of that despair and depression that come when the reign of God is on the horizon but never seems to arrive.

Lent is a moment for counting up the perceived failures in our heart and the toils of the time spent in reducing the poverty, the spoilage, the oppression, the injustice and the inequality that grow with each passing day whatever our efforts – and realising once more that all our striving was worthwhile.

Thought for the day

The effort we make to co-create the world in the design of God is the measure of our virtue and the meaning of conversion.

Prayer

Shepherd God, bring me back from my wanderings, centre my heart and settle my soul, so that no amount of failure, no measure of disappointment can deter my journey to justice, to You.

Amen.

David Adam
Holy Week

Passion/Palm Sunday

The outpouring of God

Lk 19:28-40; Is 50:4-7; Ps 21:8-9, 17-20, 23-24; Ph 2:6-11; Lk 22:14-23:56

His state was divine, yet Christ Jesus did not cling to his equality with God, but emptied himself to assume the condition of a slave.

(Philippians 2:6)

Holy Week is when we see the great love of God in action. We are made to face the God who is willing to be scorned and rejected, the God who allows himself to be counted as nothing by many. We look at the Christ who pours himself out in love.

This is a God who will not force himself upon us, it is a God who will empty himself for us: a God who will not demand his rights but one who will seek us out in love. A God who comes down to where we are, no matter how far we have fallen, who is willing to enter into the lowest place to lift us up. There is no dignity here, no standing on rights or claiming of position, only a willingness to suffer and to serve.

He does not come with an agenda or with a list of rules. He offers all he has, he offers himself, "even accepting death, death on a cross". No one can make him do this, only love. No bonds, no nails can hold him, only love. He will accept slavery to bring in the glorious liberty of the children of God. He will accept emptiness to bring us into the riches of his kingdom. He will accept death that we may have eternal life.

This week we are invited to walk the way of the cross, the way of the Suffering Servant. Whoever the original "servant" was in the Isaiah passages, we see Christ fulfilling this role.

It is a week to come down out of our own security, dignity and rights and to find ourselves in the service of others. In our sharing with the other we hear a voice that says, "As much as you did it to the least of these, you did it to me." The God who comes down will still meet us where people are down. Let us see how in the poor and the oppressed the Christ calls, how in the scorned and the rejected he is to be met.

We live in a world where it would seem you have to hold on to everything, make sure you do not lose out, win as much as you can. The aims of society seem to be prestige, prominence, promotion. The grasping society needs to hear again of he who did not snatch at his equality with God. Let us place ourselves this week where the Suffering Servant is found.

Thought for the day

If "although Jesus was rich, yet for our sakes he became poor" (2 Corinthians 8:9), how ought we who are Christians deal with the gifts and riches that God has given to us in this world of poverty? He who has more than enough should not rob him who has none.

Prayer

Lord, that I may see your face in other people's faces, that I may behold your presence in everyone I meet. That the gifts I have received may be given in the service of others.

Amen.

Monday of Holy Week

The gentleness of the Servant

Is 42:1-7; Ps 26:1-3, 13-14; Jn 12:1-11

He does not cry out or shout aloud or make his voice heard in the streets. He does not break the crushed reed nor quench the wavering flame.

(Isaiah 42:2-3)

The great problem for so many of us is the countless voices that batter our hearts and minds for attention. Claim upon claim is being made upon us.

In many parts of the world there is no gentleness, only force: you will do this or else. Doors are not knocked upon but broken down, and so, often, is the human spirit. We have learned many subtle ways of coercing and subduing others. There are many regimes that are determined to have their way.

Now and again we all try and dominate someone or something. This is not the way of the Suffering Servant: he does not publicise himself or shout until he is heard. So often he speaks in a gentle murmur, a still, small voice. It may not be loud but it is there to be heeded; it may not force us, but it asks for our reaction. The call is one of love and seeks our free response.

The call is about justice – about relationships with people. Not only the justice of the law courts – procedural justice – but also distributive justice, a justice that demands fair shares, a just sharing of resources, rights and responsibilities.

The weak and the poor, who do not have a voice, have to be protected. There has to be a gentleness that will not break people or snuff out the spirit that is within them. Sadly, much of mission has been of the conquering, imperial kind; mission has sometimes destroyed whole peoples in the name of God.

May we also now learn a new sensitivity and a new gentleness. We are to follow the Servant who does not break the crushed reed – or the crushed person – who does not quench the wavering flame or extinguish the flickering spirit. Not only will he not crush, we know he will repair; not only will he not quench, we know he will breathe into life again.

Thought for the day

The gentleness of God is needed to soften our hardness in our dealings with one another. We need to learn how to sustain the broken and the wavering without triumphing over them, for in truth we share a common lot. We are broken people who need the healing of the Christ.

Prayer

Lord, you are gentle in your dealings with me, make me gentle in my dealings with others. Grant that I may lift the fallen, ease the burdened, sustain the weak, repair the broken, for you have done all this for me in Christ my Lord.

Amen.

Tuesday of Holy Week

The call of God

Is 49:1-6; Ps 70:1-6, 15-17; Jn 13:21-33, 36-38

"It is not enough for you to be my servant to restore the tribes of Jacob and bring back the survivors of Israel. I will make you a light to the nations so that my salvation may reach to the ends of the earth."

(Isaiah 49:6)

Many people speak of vocation as if it were a one-off. You may have a vocation to be a priest, a nurse, a farmer or a mother, but I am sure that God is calling you to something even larger than any one of these.

Vocation calls us out of where we are to something new and often undreamt-of until that moment. Vocation, like life, evolves and changes. God does not call us once but many times. Few of us are called to fulfil the same work forever.

God's call is ever one that beckons us out from where we are, from our entrenched positions and our false securities, that we may take risks and brave adventures in his world. God's call is expansive and asks us to be outgoing. God's call is life-extending. God's call is not just to Jews, or Catholics or evangelicals, but to all peoples in all places at all times. It is amazing how we want to limit God to the things we want to do and the people with whom we agree.

It is too easy for the Church to get caught up in its own survival, its own renewal and restoration. These are good things and necessary, but they must not be ends in themselves. What applies to individuals applies to the Church: "He who would save his life will lose it; he who will lose his life for my sake will save it." We are called to move out. The Church is called to mission, to reach out.

At all times we are called to restoration and revival. We need renewal and rededication, but not in our "spiritual" lives only. God is concerned with the city and politics, with nations as much as with the Church. We belittle our God if we think he only wants us to work within the confines of the Church or the established order.

Salvation is not just about souls, it is also about communities and nations, about peace and justice. Sometimes this will demand sharp speaking and well-directed words. When God calls we are to respond. A person cannot serve God and keep silent when wickedness and corruption flourish.

Thought for the day

Anyone who is unwilling to face the otherness in the other person will seek to create a god in their own image. Our God is to be met in all peoples.

Prayer

Lord, extend our vision to see beyond the obvious;
Open our eyes to the wonders about us.
Open our minds to the mysteries around us.
Open our hearts to the strangers who meet us.
Open our lives to your call
That we may reach out with your love to all peoples.

Amen.

Wednesday in Holy Week

The sensitivity of the Servant

Is 50:4-9; Ps 68:8-10, 21-22, 31, 33-34; Mt 26:14-25

The Lord has given me a disciple's tongue. So that I may know how to reply to the wearied, he provides me with speech. Each morning he wakes me to hear, to listen like a disciple.

(Isaiah 50:4)

The role of the Servant is to listen, to be open, to be attentive, to be sensitive to what is going on in the world. We need to learn to listen before we speak, to understand before we dare criticise. If our ears are not sensitive to others we will seek to create them in our own image, and that is idolatry.

Too often today the attitude encouraged is one of insensitivity. We can watch the starving of the world on our television screens whilst we eat our evening meal; we can hear of the plight of the street children of our world and not be moved. Whenever this happens it is because something in us has become dulled. Our senses need to be sharpened; we need to be made aware once more.

We have become so hardened that we can be witnesses of a tragedy and not respond. We are like the western journalists who took pictures of Kenyan church leaders being beaten by the army. How different is the Servant's response: a local report of the incident simply stated that African journalists had saved a priest about to be shot. There were no pictures. They had thrown aside their cameras to run to his rescue.

The world seems to say:

"Blessed are the blind, for they do not need to see the need for action.

Blessed are the deaf, for they do not hear the cries of the poor.

Blessed are those with their feelings dulled, for they will not be moved.

Blessed are those who have hearts of stone, for they will do nothing rash."

Such thoughts cannot be for those who follow in the steps of the Suffering Servant, who gives his life as a ransom for many. We are called to give ourselves to others, and the first step along the road is learning to give our undivided attention.

We need to come to the other person without preconceived ideas and hidden agendas; we need to know who they are and where they stand. We are not to seek to recreate them in our own image. We need to listen carefully to their pleas, to hear what they hope for, to share their dreams and their fears.

Thought for the day

Whoever does not listen carefully to others can hardly claim to listen to the voice of God. One of the greatest ways of learning to hear God's voice is to learn to be attentive.

Prayer

Lord, you speak to us in the simple needs of our neighbours,
You speak to us in the great power struggles of the world,
You speak to us in the cries of the poor,
You speak to us in the damaged earth.
Give us ears to hear, hearts to love,
And wills to do what you would have us do.

Amen.

Maundy Thursday

The broken body, the wine outpoured

Ex 12:1-8, 11-14; Ps 115:12-13, 15-18; 1 Co 11:23-26; Jn 13:1-15

On the same night he was betrayed, the Lord Jesus took
some bread, and thanked God for it and broke it, and he
said, "This is my body, which is for you; do this as a
memorial of me." In the same way after supper he took the
cup and said, "This cup is the new covenant in my blood.
Whenever you drink it, do this as a memorial of me."

(1 Corinthians 11:23-25)

I was once taking a House Communion in a block of
sheltered accommodation, and as I broke the bread in two, I
looked through the gap and saw a man being carried out of
the house opposite on a stretcher. Looking at him, I said the
words of Christ, "This is my body which is for you." The
broken Christ for broken people. The heart of Christ went
out to that man on the stretcher. He may not know it, but
Christ ever offers himself for him, for you, for me. The
broken Christ is for broken people. If you are broken, come.
He is for you.

In the Eucharist we offer broken hopes and broken dreams,
broken relationships and broken hearts. Here in the bread
we offer all of our lives, our joys and our sorrows. We seek
to be one with the Christ, for he alone can make us whole –
and holy. We seek a holy union with him.

So we seek to be joined to all the broken people: the broken
in mind, the broken in body, and the broken in spirit. We
come to the Saviour that we might be ransomed, healed,
restored, forgiven. But if we cannot acknowledge our own
brokenness and if we ignore those who are broken around
us, we create a barrier to truly sharing in his offering. To
accept the broken bread is to admit brokenness in our lives,

to confess the need for a Saviour and to seek to uplift the broken in our world. Just as the Saviour was broken for us, we can only help broken people if we acknowledge our brokenness.

The cup contains wine that has been made with the crushing of the grapes, yet in the crushing and the fermenting the spirit has been set free. Let us remember that the Last Supper was celebrated in the context of the Passover. St John more than once links Jesus to Moses and the Exodus. We are moving out of slavery into liberty, out of drudgery into glory. We are on our way to the promised land. We cannot come to this land alone, we must journey together. None must be left behind in darkness.

This thought often assails me: "If we leave one person in darkness or captivity and we know of it, we will be sent back until they are free and accepted as a child of light."

Thought for the day

The atonement is what it says: we are one in him, we are not separate from him. We share a common union, but this can only be fulfilled if we are truly in communion with each other.

Prayer

Lord Jesus Christ, on the night that you were betrayed, you prayed that we might be one in you. Help us to see the unity that is ours through your love and forgiveness. We need not strive for unity, we need only accept it. We are already one in you through your redeeming love; help us to live this reality.

Amen.

Good Friday

The silent Servant

Is 52:13-53:12; Ps 30:2, 6, 12-13, 15-17, 25; Heb 4:14-16, 5:7-9;
Jn 18:1-19:42

Without beauty, without majesty we saw him, no looks to attract our eyes: a thing despised and rejected by men, a man of sorrows and familiar with suffering, a man to make people screen their faces; he was despised and we took no account of him. And yet ours were the sufferings he bore, ours the sorrows he carried.

(Isaiah 53:2-4)

There is a strangeness about this Servant passage when you realise it was written hundreds of years before the Crucifixion. It surely describes someone at the time of the prophet, as well as looking forward to the Christ. And it helps to show that joys and sorrows, hopes and fears are common to each generation.

In this passage the Servant does not speak. But the suffering one has an advocate who will not keep silent. God himself speaks at the beginning and the end, promising that he will exalt his Servant. He will vindicate, for he is concerned with this unmerited suffering. The beginning is full of hope with the promise that God will raise up. This exalting will not be in private but before all the nations.

God's power is manifested through the weakness of the Servant. Because the servant has obeyed and borne the sufferings, healing comes. Through the broken Christ on the cross we who are broken can find wholeness – this is the atonement for us all. He was wounded for our transgressions, crushed for our iniquities; by his bruises we are healed.

In the middle section the community is meditating upon the meaning of life and death, on the meaning of the one who has appeared among them and been so cruelly stricken.

It is good for us to meditate on the great mysteries of today. He who hung the earth in space is hung upon the cross. The King of kings and Lord of lords is crowned with thorns. He who gave light to the world enters darkness. He who accepts all peoples is scorned and rejected of men. He who gives life eternal accepts death. He who sets us free enters the tomb. He who created the heavens descends into hell.

Thought for the day

If the world can do this to the God of love, what might it do to us? We will be afraid unless we learn that all this is done that we can be freed from such tyranny and violence and brought into the glorious liberty of the children of God.

Prayer

Lord, we bow before the great mysteries of today.
We come before the great mystery of your love.
You give us life, you give us love,
Now we see you give us yourself,
Help us to give our lives, our love, ourselves to you,
Christ our loving Lord.

Amen.

Holy Saturday

The God who descends

One of the great statements of the creed is: "He descended into hell." In one new translation from the Latin this has become: "He descended into the grave." Now that is not enough for me! I am glad to know that God would die for me, I am relieved to know that when I descend into the grave, he has already conquered it; but I need to know he descended even further, into hell itself and all the hells of this world.

Often people will tell you that you make your own heaven and earth and your own hell. Now we know this is not true. The Scriptures are quite clear that God created heaven and earth. We are only capable of creating hell. We create hell for ourselves and for others. It is not what God wants, but he allows us to use our free will. Still, even there, where we forsake and deny him, he will not leave us or forsake us.

I need to know that when I leave him, he does not forsake me; when I ignore him, he does not ignore me. Fortunately, when I cease believing in God, he does not cease believing in me. I need to know even more, I need know he has descended into the lowest depths, because I can fall there.

When I look back over Holy Week, I know that he has experienced the hells of this world. He has been betrayed by a loved one, misunderstood by friends, forsaken by his closest companions. He has suffered bodily, spiritually and mentally. The world and evil have done their best to break him. He has felt God-forsaken. He has entered the hells of this world; he has entered into that land of nothingness beyond death that he may bring out from it all who are held captive. The Christ is like Moses bringing his people out of slavery to the promised land and he does it by descending to where they are, even if it is hell itself.

On Holy Island our lives are governed by the tide. There are a few hours every day when you cannot get off the island. Almost every week in the summer there are some visitors who will ignore all the notices and try and get across. They get caught in the sea and have to take refuge in a safety box. From there they can watch the water slowly rise around their car. If they are in real need, they can ring from this box and they will be rescued. The RAF Sea King helicopter will lower a winchman who will descend right to where they are. He comes down into their situation so that he can lift them up and bring them to safety.

When I say, "He descended into hell", I express the belief that Christ does that for me. I know that no matter how far I fall, underneath are the everlasting arms – and the hands that bear the print of the nails.

Thought for the day

No matter how far I have fallen, no matter to what depths I have descended, underneath are the everlasting arms.

Prayer

Lord, you come down among us, you come to where we are, you meet us as we are, you come down to lift us up. May you who descended into hell help us to rise to be with you in glory.

Amen.

Easter Day

The living Lord

Rm 6:3-11; Ps 117:1-2, 16-17, 22-23; Lk 24:1-12

"Why look among the dead for someone who is alive? He is not here; he has risen."

(Luke 24:5-6)

The women who followed Jesus from Galilee, Mary Magdala, Joanna, Mary the mother of James and the others, witnessed the crucifixion. They stood far off but they were there, and in heart as close as could be. They suffered with him. The women were again present at the burial. They saw how the body was laid. No doubt many hopes and dreams died with him and were buried with him.

The women were not allowed to visit the tomb on the Sabbath, so they waited until the dawn on the Sunday. Here was a new day with new hopes and promises, but it could hardly have been so for them. They wanted to pay their respects to the dead body of their dear friend. Their hearts were as heavy as the stone of the tomb as they walked carrying the spices. But they found that the stone was rolled away and soon so would the heaviness of their hearts give way to joy.

To begin with, however, the empty tomb could only cause them to be perplexed and the messengers of God only made them afraid. In St Luke's gospel the women are treated as disciples and are not told to go and tell anyone. However, they do tell the eleven and all the rest what they have experienced.

They had gone to see the dead, to attend the tomb and to embalm the body, last acts of love for a dear one departed. They were completely amazed by what happened. The glories of Easter broke unexpectedly upon them to change them forever. They learned of the risen Lord; they all wondered at that which had come to pass. We are asked to share in their wonder. Soon they will see him for themselves.

Too many treat the Christ as if he were dead, as a piece of history. He is the risen and the living Lord.

He is not to be studied, analysed and examined so much as to be met with. Too often the Church talks about him when it could be talking to him. Study groups are in danger of dissecting what is living and wondering why they are left with a corpse. He is the living Lord. He is to be met. He breaks into our darkness and fear. He wants to share with us. Faith is not a credal belief, it is a personal relationship with the living Lord.

Thought for the day

"Let him Easter in us, be a day-spring to the dimness of us." (Gerard Manley Hopkins, *The Wreck of the Deutschland*)

Prayer

Lord, risen Christ, may we find in our relationship with you
A sure ground for our faith,
A firm support for our hopes,
The ability to triumph over darkness and death,
The assurance of love everlasting,
And the sure knowledge that life is eternal.

Amen.